Advance praise for *The Tired Dad.*

"As a dad who helps dads, I'm extremely grateful for *The Tired Dad.* Where most books for dad are how-to books with varying degrees of helpfulness, *The Tired Dad* provides a much more valuable resource: community. If you're a dad, you will find yourself, your struggles, your triumphs, your doubts, your fears, and your joys in the pages of these reflections. Oftentimes, for us, the most important thing we need to hear is that we are not alone."

—Jon Fogel, creator of the Whole Parent Academy and author of *Punishment-Free Parenting*

"In a world that can make dads feel like they need to carry the weight of the world alone, *The Tired Dad* is a refreshing antidote. Every modern dad needs this book on their nightstand, in their conversations with one another, and in their hearts as they walk through the beautiful and exhausting role of fatherhood. Jon Gustin is not just helping dads feel seen. He is redefining what modern fatherhood looks like, and we are all better for it."

—Libby Ward, author of *Honest Motherhood*

"Gustin's message both tugs at my heartstrings and helps me put into perspective who I want to be as a father. For any father who is actively dealing with the addictions and distractions of life in the twenty-first century, this book centers what is actually important and gives us courage to take steps to be a dad who uses 'tired' as a badge of honor."

—Zachary Watson, coach, content creator, educator

"Gustin understands what most parenting advice misses: that you can be doing everything you're supposed to do and still feel like you're barely surviving. *The Tired Dad* meets parents in that reality without trying to fix it or add one more thing to the list. In my work helping parents understand their nervous systems and regulate past burnout, I see this every day. Gustin sees this, too, and his reflections offer something more valuable than solutions. They offer validation."

—Dr. Brooke Weinstein, nervous system regulation expert, founder and CEO of Thrive Like a Parent

"There are endless books marketed to parents but so few that speak directly to dads and the real, lived experience of fatherhood. *The Tired Dad* does just that. It's honest, tender, and deeply human. Gustin doesn't tell you how to fix or perform fatherhood; he invites you to show up fully in it. This book is the conversation so many dads have been missing."

—Alyssa Blask Campbell, MEd, *New York Times* bestselling author, researcher, and emotional development expert

"Jon Gustin understands intrinsically that parenting isn't for the weak, nor is it for the unnaturally proud. *The Tired Dad* reminds us that we are here to create a safe haven for our children and at the same time challenge them so that they will be self-sustaining when reaching adulthood. The truth is that at the same time we are challenging our own maturity during every second of that responsibility to our children—parenting is not for the weak of heart."

—Josh Brolin, actor and author of *From Under the Truck*

the tired dad.

the tired dad.

100 Reflections on Showing Up for What Matters Most

Jon Gustin

CONVERGENT
NEW YORK

Convergent
An imprint of Random House
A division of Penguin Random House LLC
1745 Broadway, New York, NY 10019
convergentbooks.com
penguinrandomhouse.com

Library of Congress Cataloging-in-Publication Data
Names: Gustin, Jon, author
Title: The tired dad / by Jon Gustin.
Description: First edition. | New York, NY: Convergent Books, [2026]
Identifiers: LCCN 2025037587 (print) | LCCN 2025037588 (ebook) | ISBN 9780593980460 hardcover | ISBN 9780593980477 ebook
Subjects: LCSH: Fatherhood | Fathers
Classification: LCC HQ756.G88 2026 (print) | LCC HQ756 (ebook)
LC record available at https://lccn.loc.gov/2025037587
LC ebook record available at https://lccn.loc.gov/2025037588

Printed in the United States of America

1st Printing

First Edition

book team: Production editor: Luke Epplin • Managing editor: Allie Fox • Production manager: Sarah Feightner • Proofreaders: Adele Starrs, Vicki Fischer, Deb Bader

Book design by Susan Turner

The authorized representative in the EU for product safety and compliance is Penguin Random House Ireland, Morrison Chambers, 32 Nassau Street, Dublin D02 YH68, Ireland.
https://eu-contact.penguin.ie

To my wife, Jessica—thank you for believing in me,
even when I didn't believe in myself.

To my daughter, Dakota, and son, Asher—never stop
dreaming, and never rush to grow up.
You are my greatest joy.

To my dad, Roy—thank you for showing me
what true character looks like.

The Child is father of the Man. . . .

—William Wordsworth, "My Heart Leaps Up"

Contents

Introduction

Becoming a Tired Dad

I'm not afraid to admit it: I'm a *tired dad.* When I was younger, saying "I'm tired" meant that I was done. I was over it. But if I thought I was tired as a kid, I had no idea how much more worn down I'd feel as a dad. I have two children who are eight and five as I write this, and if there's one thing I've learned in my parenting journey so far, it's that small children rob you of the very thing you need for brain function and overall well-being: sleep. During the day, parents are working hard on their career, relationships, childcare, household maintenance, health, and personal growth. At night, they juggle homework, bedtime, and the hope of finally getting some uninterrupted sleep.

Who can blame a dad for often feeling "over it"? Over the constant fighting between kids. Over feeling unappreciated. Over getting minimal sleep. But what if a *tired dad* has another meaning? What if it could be a positive thing to be tired?

A few years back, I started posting videos online under the handle The Tired Dad. What I'd hear from so many dads—and moms—out there is that they were tired. The videos made them feel seen in the daily challenge of being a parent. I made a sweatshirt with those two simple words printed in bold, white Helvetica font, TIRED DAD., and just about every time I wore it, people would stop me.

One time, an older man at the gym glanced at my sweatshirt, looked away, and then muttered, "I would've never worn something like that." I wasn't sure what he meant until he added, "They grow up too quick to be tired." I didn't respond, and, looking back, maybe I should have. Not to defend myself or the sweatshirt, but because he was clearly a tired dad, too, and maybe he didn't even realize it. He probably would have been surprised by what he could have learned if he'd looked beyond his own interpretations.

Another time, at a restaurant, a woman saw my sweatshirt and without hesitation said, "If you're doing it right." That simple phrase deserved a response that matched the depth of what I felt, but in the moment I only managed a quick "Absolutely." I wanted to know her story. How many kids had she raised? What struggles had she endured? What wisdom could she share? Of course, a passing comment in a restaurant isn't the time for a three-hour interview, but her words stuck with me. A quiet acknowledgment of our shared experience, the hard, beautiful work of parenting.

This book is the conversations I wish I could have had in those encounters. It's an invitation to think, reflect, and connect about the experience of being a parent. I promise you this: It's not a "how-to" book or a manual, and I'm no parenting expert. These are my reflections on fatherhood, the insights I've gained, and the ways I am challenging myself to grow alongside my children.

I'm a dad, so this book is written from a dad's perspective. Tired moms, you are absolutely welcome here. There's plenty to relate to; we're all in it together. But because of my perspective, I'll be speaking mostly to the dads. What's more, we need it. Dads are often silent strugglers. We try to figure things out alone. Which often leads to us feeling crazy and isolated. That ends here.

I'm leaving everything on the table. If you follow me online, you know that my goal is to show my authentic experience of fatherhood, with all its triumphs and failures, and that goal is the same here. My hope is that these reflections feel like an arm around your shoulder, offering encouragement, reassurance, and the reminder that you are *not alone*. You're not crazy. You're doing a good job.

These short essays are meant to be read however you need them. There are no rules. They are short, because if you're a tired dad like me, you don't have much time. You can read them in order, out of order, once, twice, or ten times. Daily, weekly, monthly, or yearly. I've included a question or suggestion at the end of each chapter that you can take or leave as you need that day. This book can sit wherever you keep the things that matter to you. Pick it up when you need it most. And when you're done, pass it on to another tired dad. That's the ultimate goal.

It's time to flip the script on being a tired dad. We are tired because we're doing it right. We're tired *from* parenting, not *of* parenting. We're tired from our most important role. We wear many hats in life, but *Dad* is the one where tiredness becomes a badge of honor. It's no longer a negative weight but a sign that we're showing up—for our children, our partners, our families, and ourselves.

Some days, we're not the happiest we've ever been, but we keep showing up. No matter what.

So, welcome. I invite you to enter the reflections of a tired dad.

the tired dad.

1

You're Not Alone, Dad

Fatherhood can be lonely. Many of us have been told we shouldn't complain, that we need to put our heads down and lead our families. That even when it's hard, even when we could use some help, no one is coming to save us. Our society has given men the message that it would rather see us die as heroes atop our white horses than watch us fall down. That's how high the expectations are. We're supposed to be heroes, not humans.

And so we buy into this message, keep riding, keep pushing, keep fighting—often doing it alone, often in the dark. I'm all for the warrior attitude, and I believe that you, Dad, can fight off a lot of these demons. I also believe some of you can't put up the fight, some won't, and some think you can until you can't. I want to validate you in whatever your struggles look like. I want to give you flowers before your funeral. I want to put my bloody fist in the air and give you a fatherly battle cry that motivates you to show up one more day.

Fellow tired dad, you are not alone in these struggles, even if it feels that way sometimes. The version of fatherhood as I experience it and that I share throughout this book may not look like yours. You may be a single dad, newly divorced, married, or soon-to-be married. You may be in a good mental space or a bad one, feeling good about where you are these days or wishing you were somewhere else. No matter the dynamic, fatherhood is hard, and there can be a severe lack of appreciation.

We have been sitting on top of our own horses, wearing our forced smiles like everything is okay, gritting our way through in the dark. This isn't what modern fatherhood should be. It's not what the future of fatherhood should be, and it's definitely not what we want to raise our sons and daughters to view as the definition of a good father. You can man up, find your identity in the masculine, push through hard times, and raise that bloody fist, but we need you here for your family. We need you here to raise the next generation. Our children, our partners—they need us fathers.

It's up to this generation of fathers to raise the torch and light the way. The last generation has played their part, and depending on the relationship you had (or didn't have) with your father, you might be feeling the lasting effects of that, and seeing it seep into your own parenting. But it's our turn now. We can change narratives, expectations, and definitions of what it means to be a man. Tired? Of course you are. You're a hardworking dad who has the world on his back. The good news is you don't have to do it alone: There are more support groups, online therapists, and people to connect with now than ever before. Find your tribe. Diminish your fears of vulnerability and self-healing. That's manning up. Stare at those wounded parts and do the work to heal, not just cover them up.

Help me in becoming a voice for fathers. This is a call for duty. If you are fortunate enough to have found a person, a partner, who helps you off that horse to give you a drink of water, protect that person with everything you have. And whether you have a supportive partner or not, find your tribe. You aren't alone, Dad. It's just quiet in the dark. Get off your horse, light your torch, and follow me on this journey.

What battle are you fighting, alone and in the dark? There's no shame in seeking out professional help.

(See page 233 for a list of resources.)

2

The New Dad Era

Welcome to the New Dad Era. Gone are the days when the main role dads were expected to play was the financial provider for the family. Now dads are actively involved with all aspects of parenting and home life.

The modern dad isn't an authoritarian. He's engaged, walking through life with his children. He validates their feelings and encourages them to express emotion, communicate openly, stay true to themselves, and never give up.

The modern dad understands the importance of quality time with his kids. Even if he works long hours, he's fully committed to being a dad when he clocks out. We're not fathers who just exist in the home; we're the engine that makes it run. We immerse ourselves in every facet of family life.

The modern dad shows up—not with a checklist of

chores, but with a shared mindset: "What needs to be done?" It's not about splitting tasks 50/50 or assigning roles. It's about stepping in, being aware, and doing our part to create a home rooted in love, support, and growth.

Because while dads are more present than ever, the truth is—moms still carry a lot. The goal isn't perfection, it's partnership. It's noticing the invisible work, lightening the load, and building a space where everyone thrives. A household where raising good humans isn't just the goal. It's the natural outcome.

Before my daughter was born, a co-worker said to me: "You're either going to be a good dad or a bum dad. Being a bum dad is easy—it's the easy way out."

Naturally, I knew I didn't want to be a bum dad. Part of me feared I wouldn't measure up. Was I ready for this? Of course not. No one is ever fully ready for something they've never experienced. People told me it would be different—in the best way. That it would be hard, possibly the hardest thing in my life, but also amazing. What kind of advice is that?

Now I get it. I'm tired, but I'm the happiest I've ever been. We don't usually equate tiredness with happiness. When I've been tired from a job I hated, it led to burnout. But when I was tired from a hobby I loved, a passion I poured myself into, that tiredness was easily ignored, overshadowed by pure joy. The moment my firstborn entered the world, the happiness I felt surpassed all my passions, interests, hobbies, and nostalgic childhood memories combined. It was *uncharted* tiredness, but also *uncharted* happiness.

This is the new era of tired dads. So, what kind of dad do you choose to be?

Write or think about three words that describe what being a modern dad means to you.

3

The Measure of a Good Dad

When my daughter was five years old, she asked me to have a tea party with her. I was running around trying to get some work done on a deadline, so I told her I didn't have time. I can still see the disappointed look on her face.

Some days, I feel like I'm hitting the mark of what it means to be a good dad. Other days, like that tea party day, not so much. These moments of parenthood are undeniably fleeting. There are days when I look at my kids and think about how many times I was busy and missed the little things. Sometimes I enter a mental spiral of everything I've done wrong, and feel the guilt crushing me. When my daughter asked me to join her tea party, should I have stopped what I was doing, called off work, and joined in? Of course, the answer depends on so many things—if I'm under a deadline at work, if she can wait until later that day, if this is the first tea party I've said no to this week or the tenth. If my standard as a good dad is being present in my kids' lives, there are going to be days when I don't meet that standard. And it's true for us all. No matter how much we try to do the right thing, there are times we are going to fall short—at least to our standards. We're never going to measure up. Why? Because we're good fathers.

If you're going to take anything from this book, remember that. Sure, there are going to be those moments when we say, "I messed up. I need to do better." There are days when we're distracted or stressed—we're all humans with responsibilities—and even though we would like to enjoy a never-ending bliss of tea parties, it isn't realistic. Moments will come and go, and there's nothing we can do about it. We snatch at them as they whoosh by, hoping to grab as many good ones as we can.

If you feel guilty in some of these situations, you need to hear that it's actually because you're a good parent. Bad parents don't feel guilty about this. Bad parents don't put their kids first. Bad parents don't wonder whether they're doing a good job or how they could improve.

You're not a bad parent. You're not a bad father. This is the measure of a good dad.

Write it down or just say it aloud: "I'm a good dad." Now believe it.

4

The Mirror

Life is a mirror and will reflect back
to the thinker what he thinks into it.
—Ernest Holmes

When my daughter entered the world, it felt as if a mirror had been placed in front of my life. Suddenly, every unhealed part of myself was exposed. I realized I needed to heal—not just for me, but for her.

Have you ever had this experience? I'm talking about facing the deep-rooted emotional stuff. Stripping away all the crutches and confronting our challenges head-on can be terrifying. It's some of the hardest work you'll ever do.

Two voices will always be there, pulling you in opposite directions—the angel and the devil on your shoulders. One voice will tell you exactly what you want to hear. It's comforting and tempting because it requires no effort. "You're fine just the way you are," it whispers. "Let the world accept you for the amazing person you already are." That's the devil.

The other voice tells you what you don't want to hear. It says there's work to do. Deep down, you know you haven't healed those parts, but you've gotten really good at keeping them buried in the basement. Surely, they'll never surface. Except, some already have. You've just mastered hiding them from the world. Maybe your partner sees them but looks the other way. Maybe there's been an ultimatum: Fix it or lose something precious.

It's like a wrestling match with yourself—a constant battle between these two voices, both of which make sense in the moment. Some things that surface may be rooted in wounds from childhood, and those "basement dwellers" may start clawing their way out. When you face these unhealed parts of yourself, you have a choice: Accept that there's work to be done or deny there's anything wrong. So, what's it going to be?

You know the answer. No one said it would be easy. Those basement dwellers gained strength in the dark. They've been fed well. But so have you.

When you face the mirror and resist the tempting voice offering an easier way out, you begin to uncover who you truly are and why you do the things you do. The sooner you start the work—the real healing work, not just slapping on Band-Aids or shoving things back into the basement—the better. Because we have children now. The stakes are higher. Those basement dwellers can't grow stronger. We have other souls to protect, guide, and nurture—to help them become a version of themselves that's free from the burdens gazing back at us.

We all have these reflections. Some are darker than others. We all have a past, a story, and a desire to give our children the best. This is part of that process.

It may feel like this journey of fatherhood isn't about you anymore, but it is. You know how a mirror reflects light onto other surfaces? That light will reflect onto our children.

You won't heal overnight, but starting the journey—acknowledging the need for it—is what matters most. Complete healing might not come, but the progress will make you better than the person who first looked into that mirror.

What do you need to face when you look into the mirror? Reflect on that today and take the first step toward dealing with it.

5

Keep Showing Up

Do you ever look around at all the good things in your life and know you *should* feel happy but can't seem to feel it? Five years ago, I was feeling lost as a husband and as a father. Approaching my mid-thirties, I argued with my wife often, my finances weren't where I wanted them to be, and I didn't feel I was at the place in my life I should be. I felt like I was drowning, like I had no clear direction. As a result, I started getting too close to my backstabbing, lying friend—alcohol. I made mistakes. I wasn't always present. I let my temper get the better of me at times. What saved me was when I decided I would *keep showing up.* No matter how imperfectly I did it, all that mattered was that I showed up. I wrote the mantra down and looked at it every day.

Now it's your turn. Has today been a bad day? Horrible day? Worst day ever?

Are you struggling with your mental health? Did you lose your temper . . . again?

Maybe it was a good day? Amazing day? Best day ever.

Keep showing up. No matter what.

Keep showing up is a simple phrase, yet it encapsulates the commitment and love that fatherhood demands. It means being there for your children day in and day out, regardless of personal struggles or setbacks. It signifies that even on the toughest days, when your patience wears thin or the weight of life's challenges feels overwhelming, you persevere.

Keep showing up is a mantra of dedication. It's about accepting that there's no such thing as a perfect parent. Instead, it reminds us that we imperfectly show up every day, admit our mistakes, and never give up. It's the enduring effort invested in fatherhood that will ultimately yield the rewards of a stronger, healthier family bond and having a front row seat to watch our kids grow into kind, resilient, and good human beings.

Write "keep showing up" on a piece of paper and put it somewhere (your home, car, work) to remind yourself on a regular basis.

6

Anger Is Not a Superpower

Growing up, I thought that anger was my superpower. I had been raised to see anger as a marker of strength, to believe that anger made me a man. Men have to be ready for battle at any moment, so why not carry the weapons on your shoulders every day? I saw myself as a warrior—a chaotic, unpredictable, reckless warrior. In reality, as I'd come to learn, I was overcompensating for my insecurity, immaturity, and lack of emotional intelligence.

Anger isn't a superpower. It's an emotion—a reaction—something normal. It can light a fire inside you to do something positive, to drive change. That's different from using anger as a way to avoid other emotions or feelings. When frustration or sadness arises, trying to burn the world down isn't strength. It's lunacy, not manhood. Control of one's emotions, humility, and gentleness are the real marks of strength in a man.

When I argue with my wife in front of my kids, I make a conscious effort to keep my anger in check. When my son accidentally makes a mess, or my daughter makes the same mistake for the thousandth time, I take a breath before responding. Do I always act calmly, always respond rationally? No! Have I failed at times? Of course. But I constantly remind myself that if I frequently show them my anger response, my kids will grow up thinking that's the way men should respond and act.

I want to show my son that men can be patient, gentle, and sensitive.

I want my daughter to grow up expecting those traits in the men around her, setting the standard that true strength lies in emotional control and kindness.

It's our responsibility as fathers to set that standard for the next generation of both men and women.

Find something that helps release anger in a positive way. Deadlifts with a trap bar are my favorite.

7

Choose Where You Will Focus

Have you ever heard someone say, "I'm a really bad friend," as a way of admitting they aren't great at showing up to events, returning calls, or meeting for coffee? I actually love that honesty, because many times, it shows how the person is prioritizing their life.

I also appreciate it because I know that my wife and I aren't always great friends to others. Not that I wouldn't be there for a friend in a crisis or if they needed someone to talk to. But I've decided I want to be able to focus my time and energy on the things that I prioritize in my life, which includes my work and my family. And as a result, I won't always have time to spend with my friends.

As my kids grow older and become more independent, I know I'll have more time for friends, hobbies, and other pursuits. But right now, in this stage, I prioritize my relationship with my family above everything else.

If you're thinking that sounds harsh, or that it is too hard to limit your priorities, or that it would mean closing yourself off to things and people you value, see if this reframe helps. Prioritizing just a couple of categories in our lives allows us to be *great* at them. If you wanted to learn a new language and started taking lessons in Spanish, French, and Mandarin, you might learn some new words in each, but you wouldn't learn enough to have a conversation until you chose one to focus on. If we spread ourselves too thin across too many categories, we'll be mediocre at best and I have no desire to be mediocre at my job, or with my wife and kids. I choose to be great.

It's up to you to choose where you will focus.

Is it clear to you what you prioritize in your life? Are family and work the first two categories that come to mind? Take a minute to reflect on this today.

8

Taking Ownership

I was hammered at my daughter's third birthday party. Leading up to it, I was stressed, I was tired, and then we had a social event where there would be alcohol for the adults. Deep down, I knew I wasn't being the best dad I could be in that moment, but I latched on to the excuse of "Parenting is hard. Who can blame me for having a few drinks to make it easier?"

Sometimes people say, "No matter what, you're doing enough as a parent. You may have messed up, but it's all good." To a certain extent, I agree. Parenting is messy, exhausting, and full of moments when we question ourselves. But sometimes, those sentiments gloss over something important: the need to take a hard look at ourselves and be honest when we're not showing up the way we want to.

Grace is important. It gives us room to recover when we falter. But grace without accountability keeps us stuck. It's one thing to forgive yourself for messing up; it's another to ignore the patterns that need to change.

Maybe you've been losing your temper too often. Maybe you're leaning on alcohol or other vices to cope. Maybe you're zoning out when your kids need you or letting unresolved stress and anger spill over into your parenting. I've been there (at my child's birthday party, no less). It's easier to justify those moments as normal parenting struggles, but just like I felt that day at the birthday party, deep down, we know when something isn't right.

Kids need parents who are honest with themselves and are willing to grow. They need to see us admit when we're wrong and take steps to make it right. Whether it's seeking help, cutting back on unhealthy habits, or learning healthier ways to cope, those actions matter. They show we're willing to take ownership for our mistakes. So even if it seems too hard to face down our demons, isn't it worth the effort if it shows our kids how to someday face their own challenges?

When we grow, we don't just become better parents, we teach our kids how to face their own struggles with honesty and resilience. And that's a lesson they'll carry with them forever.

What do you need to change about your lifestyle or habits? How would that change the way you interact with your kids?

9

Marriage After Kids

Having children will absolutely change your relationship with your spouse or partner—and there's no way to avoid this change. After my first child was born, I struggled with how to be an involved dad and husband, which led my marriage into a storm. A beautiful storm my wife and I thought we were prepared for, but the downpours were a little heavier than expected.

This human being we created gave our life new meaning and purpose. This human being also started pushing us apart. Did I love this new creation more than my wife? Did she love our new child more than me? Why did we begin to resent each other over things that we previously brushed away? I started creating narratives in my head that made me a victim of my wife's irrational behaviors. I was a father now, my life changed too, I had needs and I deserved better treatment. This was about my comfort, and why didn't my wife understand this? This was my ego. This was my pride. This was my immaturity in this new journey called parenthood. My wife had her own ego she was battling as well.

Over time, those small, selfish choices started adding up. We were making little cuts to our marriage that were eventually going to slice deep enough to leave a scar. Something had to give.

That "something" was our ego and pride. I got tired of fighting for my ego. The thing with ego is it's never fulfilled. It's an endless cup of self-absorption that blurs your vision to what others need from you. My wife needed me, and I was swimming neck-deep in that egotistical sludge. We both started putting in sincere effort, practicing humility, and really trying to understand each other's needs. We sat down and had an honest conversation, refused to get defensive, and when we finally listened to each other, we realized we both just needed help. I took our daughter out of the house as often as I could so my wife had some time to herself to replenish. Any parent of a newborn will agree: taking a long, uninterrupted shower is glorious and an hour-long nap is more effective than coffee. We alternated who did bedtime so the other could have some alone time. Our team was created. That shift transformed our relationship into a stronger, more fulfilling partnership.

It's easy to mourn what your marriage looked like before you had kids. But I'd encourage you not to view the change as a burial—it should be a rebirth. Just as your child is entering this world, you and your partner are entering a new stage of your marriage. It's filled with new stressors, new ways of doing things, new sacrifices—a new life that can either bring you closer together or cause you to drift further apart. Rebirth is about intentionally adapting to this new life together, creating something even stronger than what came before.

Having a child won't *fix* a struggling marriage, I feel it's important to add. Get the help your relationship needs first, because adding a child, and all the sacrifices, changes, and responsibilities that come with it will only be harder on you both.

Don't cling to what your relationship used to be. Focus on building something new—together.

Are you mourning something that has changed in your marriage? What is something small you can do today to focus on building something new instead?

10

Music in Utero

From the moment my wife and I found out we were pregnant, I knew I wanted to be active in shaping who my kids would become. I'd heard about people who played music for their kids while they were in utero, and as someone who deeply loves music, I jumped on this. Obviously, the first song I played to my unborn daughter was "Heart-Shaped Box," from Nirvana's album *In Utero* (How perfect is that?). I passionately told my wife all about how awesome the song and album were, as we held the speaker up to her belly, and although she'd roll her eyes in jest, she understood it was important to me.

I will never have the connection my wife had with our children while they were growing inside her. I still marvel at the fact that her body went through immense change to produce the perfect nutrients and safe environment for their growing bodies and minds. It was amazing to watch from the outside, but I wanted a connection with them too. I did that through music—an art form I truly feel is from our souls, the ultimate form of self-expression and feeling. And so I played lullaby renditions of songs by bands like Metallica, Nirvana, Beastie Boys, Pearl Jam, Eminem, Elton John, and so many others. I made sure to add in Mozart, Beethoven, and other classical giants for good measure.

Sharing the music that has formed my life was my very first connection with my kids. Today, I continue to share that passion with them, except now, we can sing together, dance together, and share the instruments that touch our souls.

If you have the opportunity, share the music that has been meaningful in your life with your children in utero. And continue to share with them as they grow up.

11

The Power of Perspective

We all need a perspective check sometimes. It's so easy to get caught up in all the small details and to-dos of daily life that, occasionally, we need the kind of perspective check that punches us square in the mouth.

The other day, as I was feeling stressed about getting the kids off to school and worried about a work deadline, I came across a video online that stopped me in my tracks.

It was of a child, maybe seven years old, belly-laughing on a trampoline with their family. The child's smile lit up the frame, every moment full of joy. Beneath the video, the caption read: *"POV: You're a child enjoying your last moments before transitioning to Heaven in two days."*

Beneath it, I saw this comment: *"Imagine, as the parent, the patience you'd have. How your outside worries wouldn't matter anymore."*

That's the kind of perspective I needed that day. The kind that stops time and clears the noise. Suddenly, it was okay if all the puzzle pieces in my life stayed out of place, and it didn't matter if the puzzle ever got finished. I was just grateful my puzzle *could* wait. I took a breath and understood that this moment I was in was a gift.

We can't carry heavy stories like that every day. It would crush us. And it's okay to acknowledge our problems without feeling constant guilt because someone else has it worse. Your pain, your stress—they are valid and deserve care. But sometimes, perspective *can* be the salve that clears the static in our heads. It doesn't erase challenges, but it softens their edges. It reminds us that this moment—this messy, complicated moment—is part of a bigger plan.

Cultivating a healthy perspective every day can change everything. It can change how we treat our partners, how we respond to our kids, and how we shoulder life's weight. Even something as small as pausing to appreciate the laughter in your home or the warmth of a hug can remind you that these are the moments worth holding on to.

Perspective doesn't make our problems disappear, but it reminds us that life's imperfections are often where the meaning lies.

Because this moment—right now—is all we have.

And it's beautiful.

Think about what's weighing on you today. How can you add some healthy perspective into your situation right now?

12

Vulnerability Is Freedom

When you hear the word *vulnerability,* what comes to mind? For many men, vulnerability has been portrayed as being overly emotional, which is often equated to weakness. And while expressing emotion is sometimes what vulnerability looks like, more often than not being vulnerable means being honest with ourselves and others about something challenging that we're experiencing.

When I admitted to myself that I had a drinking problem, and that it wasn't going to get better, I battled so many fears about how others would view me. Would they hold it against me? Would they be able to trust me—the guy who couldn't control his drinking? But I came to find out there were so many others who were struggling too. It wasn't until I shared what I was going through that others felt safe enough to share their own battles.

I know how scary being vulnerable can be. You're opening yourself up to criticism, hurt, and judgment. The armor comes off, and you're left with nothing—just exposure. And you can't control how others will react.

But with vulnerability comes freedom. It releases you, and it can release others. The fears that prevent others from letting their guards down are the same fears you have. The first person to drop the sword, put their arms out, and stop fighting makes others feel less alone. One of the most amazing things that happened after I shared my sobriety journey with a few close friends and then on social media was the messages I received. Some came from strangers, others from people I hadn't talked to in years. Each opened up about their own struggles with various substances. I saw firsthand how sometimes you can be the final confirmation someone needs to make a life-changing decision.

Don't underestimate the bravery it takes to be vulnerable. Being vulnerable doesn't mean that you aren't a leader or that you lack strength in handling inner turmoil. When you show vulnerability, you also give your kids permission to do the same. It builds trust, deepens empathy, and creates a home where everyone feels safe to be their truest self. You're showing your kids that it's normal—even for you, their *Superman*—to struggle. And then you show them how to beat those struggles.

What are you holding a shield up to? What's something you can do to let that armor down a bit?

13

A Life of Meaning

Succeeding in our careers, making money, and providing for our families are important parts of life, but when we put more meaning into them than we should—or even worse, make them our whole identity—that's when they bring stress. We can get too focused on asking *why:* Why aren't we higher up in the company? Why didn't we get that raise or bonus? Why does our neighbor have a nicer car? We stay up at night buried in what-ifs that most likely will never happen, placing too much meaning on flawed systems, other people's lives, and material items.

We should absolutely pursue goals, aspirations, and careers that fulfill us. But we should also find fulfillment in meaning that comes from outside of those pursuits. Instead of asking *why,* focus on the *what:* spending quality time on something that matters to you. This could look like taking a walk with your family, identifying birds, splashing in streams, or admiring a sunset. Maybe it's going to a concert, writing in your journal, or doing a hobby. Have a deep conversation, dance with your spouse in the kitchen, spend a few extra minutes at bedtime to hear about your child's day. Put value on what is truly valuable: your life.

When things get tough and you feel the weight of the world pressing down on you, take a deep breath. Look into the distance. Play with your children. Get outside. Have a good conversation. Filling your cup with the most meaningful things in life will allow you to take on the parts that are necessary without the added stress.

What is causing stress in your life right now? What is one thing you can focus on in these moments that brings meaning to your life?

14

Raising a Daughter

In June 2015, I found out my firstborn child was going to be a girl. I discovered this by getting pink silly string sprayed onto my head while wearing a blue top hat and a matching blue shirt. You can probably guess I was on Team Boy. I understood boys, having been one myself, and I wanted to give my little boy everything I had needed as a kid. Also, I assumed boys were easier to raise. Make them strong, resilient, teach them sports, and voilà—you have a man.

But I wasn't having a boy. I was having a girl—a complicated, emotionally intricate girl who would one day venture out into the world and face its challenges. The thought of not being able to protect her from the subtle ways the world diminishes innocence filled me with fear. How would I shield her from monsters?

I saw what can happen to girls in a world that doesn't

value them as it should. I'd heard the stories, witnessed the disrespect, and knew how her spark could be extinguished in quiet, insidious ways. Now I was going to raise a daughter in that world. At first, I thought I'd do what dads with daughters are "supposed" to do—get jacked, collect guns, and learn every form of self-defense imaginable. I'd joke about how she wasn't allowed to date until she was forty. That's what dads do, right?

But it didn't take long to realize how simplistic and shallow that view was.

My daughter has changed my life and the way I understand what it really means to raise a child—especially a girl. I still believe girls are complicated and emotionally complex, but I've learned those traits are not weaknesses, they're strengths. Once I let go of my preconceptions, I realized I didn't need an arsenal to prepare her for the world. I needed to encourage her to *build her own*.

She needs an internal toolbox of strength, confidence, emotional intelligence, perseverance, and the courage to unapologetically pursue her path. She needs to know how to demand respect, treat others with kindness, and carry herself with both compassion and strength. These qualities will make her not just ready for the world, but *good for it*.

For three years, my wife and I had only our daughter. Those years were filled with tea parties, Minnie Mouse, princess dresses, music, and art. She loves music. She loves art. She is—and always has been—the sweetest, most innocent little girl. It was easy to go soft on her, I thought. That's what girl dads do, right? If I'd had a boy, I'd be tougher, right?

But over time, I've realized that raising a daughter—or a son—isn't about leaning into stereotypes or letting preconceived notions guide the way. It's about raising good humans. Humans who are strong enough to handle life's challenges and kind enough to make the world a better place.

Maybe raising boys and girls isn't so different after all. Maybe the goal is the same: to give them the tools to thrive in the world, and the heart to make it better.

If you have a daughter, what is the most important thing you are doing to build a strong, deep relationship with her, one that will last forever?

15

Parent or Friend?

People say a parent should not be their child's friend. I disagree. While I am my children's parent first, I absolutely believe I should be their friend as well, and not just any friend, but their best friend.

Think for a moment about how you'd describe each role. A parent offers guidance, discipline, and love. A real, genuine friend isn't afraid to give you full honesty. They hold you accountable. They defend you. They are loyal to you, no matter what. They love you and want what's best for you. When you look at the roles side by side, you see there's not as big of a difference as we may think.

Yes, you are their parent first, in charge of their well-being and guiding them from a place of experience and perspective. But this is the New Dad Era—we aren't engaging with our kids' questions with authoritarian, right-from-wrong, my-way-or-the-highway answers. When your children come to you, they often already know whether something they did or want to do is wrong. If they don't, they are seeking an explanation—a deeper understanding from the person they respect most. If we respond with blanket statements, judgment, or the overused non-guidance of "Because I said so," or "Because it's wrong," they will begin to confide in us less and less. They will look elsewhere for explanations and understanding. You missed your shot, Dad.

As a parent, you are the best kind of friend your child could have. You always have their best interests in mind, and they can lean on you when things get tough. Connecting is better than lecturing. Be their parent, but also embody the qualities of the greatest friend they will ever have. If you are only a parent to your children, you're missing out on half of what it means to be a dad.

Have you resisted talking to your kid(s) about a particular subject, or have you held them at arm's length in any particular way? Think about these areas of your relationship and how you might deepen the connection.

16

I'm Not Liked Because You Are Loved

I recently had a conversation with a family friend whose kids have grown up, moved out, and started families of their own. Over the years, I watched his kids develop and noticed the beautiful relationship they had with their parents. His oldest, his daughter, always had such a comfortable relationship with both her father and her mother. She expressed herself openly, and I never saw judgment or discouragement from her parents—only unconditional love. The same was true for my friend's son.

This family brought so much joy to my life when I was younger. I spent a few holidays with them and loved being around their dynamic. Of course, no one is perfect, and I'm sure they've made mistakes I didn't see. But to me, they were an amazing family, the kind I dreamed of having one day.

Now a father myself, I asked this friend, "What's one piece of advice you can give me as my children prepare to enter their adolescent years?"

"No matter how strong your relationship is, difficulty will come," he began. "There will be pushback, and there will be times when your children don't like you." What he said next hit me so profoundly. "When my kids were teenagers, I would tell them, 'I love you so much, I'm willing to not be liked by you right now.' And then I stood my ground when it was the right thing to do, even if it was hard."

He went on to share how he tried to be so involved in his kids' lives that there was nothing they did he wasn't aware of. "Meet their friends, meet their friends' parents, and even meet their friends' friends' parents. Be involved when they're young—not to make decisions for them, but to guide them. Be present for the heart that lives outside your own body."

I was stunned by these words, and understanding washed over me. Yes. These are our children we're talking about. Children who will have to navigate life without us one day. Our children will face the real world—how are we preparing them for that?

We need to let our children fly, but make sure we've checked their wings first. Give them tools, but make sure they're the right ones. How we prepare our children is crucial.

What is the best parenting advice you've ever heard? What parenting advice would you give to another dad?

17

No Fear Here

Here's to raising children who don't need to change who they truly are to be accepted by their own families.

Here's to raising children who aren't silenced but can freely and safely share their voices without fearing their parents' reactions.

Here's to raising children who don't have to find themselves later because they never lost who they were in the first place.

For generations, many of us grew up in homes where fear of disappointing our parents outweighed our desire to be honest with them. We tiptoed around expressing who we were, worried about being misunderstood or dismissed. But it doesn't have to be that way anymore.

Imagine your child walking into the world with the full confidence that their family is their foundation, not a force they have to fight against. Imagine them knowing they can come to you with anything—a broken heart, a mistake they made, or a dream that feels too big to hold alone—and be met with love, not judgment.

Raising children free of fear doesn't mean there's no discipline. It means discipline is rooted in guidance, not punishment. It means teaching accountability without shame. It means building a home where children feel safe enough to fail, secure enough to grow, and loved enough to know they *are* enough.

When our children are free to be themselves, we give them the greatest gift: the freedom to step into the world authentically. They don't have to seek acceptance because they've always had it. They don't have to unravel decades of doubt because they never learned to doubt their worth.

So here's to us, the dads who break the cycle. Here's to creating homes where love and respect drown out fear. Homes where our kids can breathe deeply, speak freely, and dream wildly. Because if there's no fear here, there's only room for growth, connection, and the kind of bond that lasts a lifetime.

What can you do to let your kid(s) know that they are free to be fully and totally themselves in your presence?

18

Raising a Son

In June of 2019, I found out my second child was going to be a boy. This time, there was no pink or blue silly string—just the quiet surprise of an ultrasound screen showing my son. I was ecstatic. I would get to experience being both a girl dad and a boy dad. I had spent the past two years fully immersed in tea parties, princess dresses, and art projects. Now I was stepping into unfamiliar territory. Raising a boy.

When my son arrived, I still held the notion that boys were easier. After all, I knew what it meant to be a boy. But as the months went on, I started to realize I didn't have it all figured out. Sure, I'd grown up as a boy, but I was raising one in a very different world.

It didn't take long for me to see the parallels. First, the miracle of that first cry—it hit just as hard as it had when my daughter was born. He was tiny and fragile, just like my daughter had been. He relied on me for everything, just like she had. And as he grew, I realized something I hadn't expected: Raising him wasn't about making him "strong" or "tough." It was about teaching him to be human.

I had the same emotional connection to him as I did to my daughter. He was the sweetest boy. I had intended to be harder on him, but it turned out I didn't want to be. He was my child. I loved him just as deeply as my daughter, and I had an innate desire to protect and raise them both with the same care.

Society places boys in a box, telling them: "Don't cry," and "Be tough," and "Man up." But I didn't want to raise my son that way. I didn't want to teach him to build walls around his emotions, hide parts of himself to fit a mold, or lean on old ideas of toughness as preparation for the world. Instead, I wanted to give him the skills to be *himself*. I wanted him to know it's okay to be unguarded, to express his feelings, to care for others, and to carry kindness in his heart.

Raising my boy, like raising my girl, became less about preparing him for outdated preconceptions and more about helping him build the internal strength to navigate a complex world. It's about showing him that strength isn't the absence of fear or weakness—it's knowing how to keep going in spite of it.

My son has taught me so much. He's curious, adventurous, and fearless in a way that inspires me to encourage his independence, even when my instinct is to protect him from every scrape and bruise. His energy reminds me to loosen my grip and trust his ability to explore the world, while his gentleness reminds me to nurture his heart. He asks for hugs, tells me he loves me, and cries when his feelings are hurt. He reminds me every day that being a boy doesn't mean fitting into a box—it means embracing who you are.

I have the privilege of raising both a daughter and a son. And while their journeys may look different on the surface, the destination is the same. I want them both to be kind, confident, and strong in their own unique ways. I want them to know their worth and to treat others with the respect and compassion they deserve.

Give yourself permission to love on your little guy(s). Kiss them, hug them, and let them know how dads show affection. The world is better with secure men.

If you have a son, what's most important to you when it comes to raising him?

19

We Have This Moment

If there ever comes a day when we can't be together, keep me in your heart. I'll stay there forever.

—WINNIE-THE-POOH

My wife and I divide and conquer the bedtime routine. When I put our son to bed, she puts our daughter to bed, and then we switch the next night. We also make a point to spend some extra time with them at bedtime. When my daughter was little, I'd read a book, sing some songs, and then lie on the floor next to her crib until she fell asleep. Now our routine consists of conversations. She gives me a recap of her day: what's bothering her, her aspirations, and my favorite, her profound realizations on life as an eight-year-old. As we both stare at the ceiling, lit up by various night-lights and glow-in-the-dark stars, I listen to her spout wisdom that seems to come from some alternate universe.

Sometimes, she asks tough questions I don't have

direct answers to: "Why can't we always live together?" "Why do we have to die?" Having these types of conversations at the end of the night ensures that I won't be getting to sleep anytime soon. I answer with a question: "What do you think?" I've found this is how I get the best answers. Some reveal her innocence, while others are wiser than anything I could have said.

Case in point: Last Christmas, she wrote a wish list to send to the North Pole. Later that evening, when I secretly opened it, I saw she had written, "To spend Christmas with just my family." Here I was, thinking she'd be asking for a Barbie Dreamhouse, but no—just a wish to spend time with her family.

Children don't ever want good things to end. Neither do adults—we've just lived long enough to know the reality that they do. But children can't understand why they have to stop playing the game they're having so much fun with, or why the vacation has to end, or why in the world there's a point in life when we have to say goodbye to each other forever.

I don't have all the answers, baby girl, but I know what we do have. We have this moment, and hopefully many moments to come. We will make the best of those moments, and they'll turn into memories. My wish is that, even though the moments won't last forever, the memories we make will. And we'll always have those, no matter who's here or who's not.

At bedtime, ask your child to give you a "thumbs-up" moment and a "thumbs-down" moment from their day, appreciating the moment.

20

We Aren't Showing Up Perfectly

Most nights, I mentally run over everything that happened that day, wondering if I did enough. Did I show up the way my kids needed me to? Did I bring work home with me? Did my kids feel my stress? Did I give my wife what she needed from me? Do I feel good about the father and husband I was today? I'm not sure there has ever been a day I answered yes to all those questions. Instead of feeling bad about that, I've learned to accept that it's okay to not get it all right. The reality is we're not always going to get it right. That's not what makes us good parents. What makes us good parents is that when we get it wrong, we can admit it. We learn from it.

Perfection is not the goal. We aren't showing up perfectly, but we *are* showing up. *Keep showing up.* To be cherished in your children's memories tomorrow, be present today. Be present in the little things—the belly laughs over breakfast, the hugs that wipe away tears, and the bedtime stories that provide their comfort. It's in being there, truly there, during the victories and the meltdowns, showing them they're not alone. We all stumble. There will be days when our patience wears thin and our best intentions fall short. We learn, we grow, and eventually we find firmer ground.

So when the day ends and you question whether you did enough, remember that perfection isn't the goal. Your efforts, your love, and your commitment to showing up, even on the hard days, are what make you an incredible parent.

We aren't going to get it all right. But I want you to write down one thing you did get right today. Just one thing.

21

Eighteen Summers

When our children are young, we often hear that we have "eighteen summers" with them, a sentiment that can feel overwhelmingly sad, like a clock ticking down to a forever goodbye. And so, to make the most of it, we pack these summers with vacations and experiences, many times going back into the fall exhausted and, frankly, tired of one another!

We do all of this because, as parents, we value spending time together as a family and creating special memories. While trips and vacations can be fun, I'd encourage you to start by focusing on your home. Look at these first eighteen summers, these first eighteen years, as an opportunity to build connections and create a *home* full of love and encouragement.

If you create the comfort of a home, no matter what

your children go on to do in life, no matter whether they settle down close to home or thousands of miles away, they will always have those memories. They'll remember the home where they were free to be themselves. The home where they didn't have to hide away in their rooms to avoid being judged, criticized, or told they were lazy. A home where messes were welcome because creativity was encouraged. A home they'll reminisce about—spending summers chasing the ice-cream truck, splashing at sun-soaked pool parties, staying up late to watch movies on a weeknight. It doesn't have to be lavish or expensive, these simple family adventures can look like roasting marshmallows, playing hide-and-seek outside with neighbors, or catching bugs.

Your children will always remember how home made them feel. If done right, it will be a feeling they want to come back to, and a feeling they'll want to create for their own families. A friend of mine is a grown woman, but she still eats lunch with her dad every week, because he made it a point to make his home a place she wants to return to, and spending time with him is a happy experience.

We have eighteen years to build our home, and our kids should have until our last breath to feel welcome in it.

What's one childhood memory about home that sticks out to you? Whatever it is, re-create it for your children.

22

Be the First Person to Compliment Your Children

The other day, my son brought me a picture he had drawn. "Oh wow," I said, "I see how hard you worked on this. I love it, buddy!" Seeing the joy on his face reminded me how I always want to be the first person to compliment my children. I don't want them to hear from others what I should have been telling them all along: that I'm proud of them. Some kids go their entire lives without ever hearing those words from their parents.

Think back to your own childhood. Did your parents make you feel seen and valued? Or were compliments scarce, leaving you to question your worth? If you were lucky enough to grow up in a home filled with encouragement, you know the power of those words. If not, you know how much they were missed. Either way, you have the chance to shape a different narrative for your own kids.

We often talk about the toxic things parents say to their children, but sometimes the most harmful thing is what they *don't* say. The silence can be deafening. A lack of acknowledgment or praise can leave children filling in the blanks themselves, often with doubt and insecurity. When children grow up without hearing affirmations like "I'm proud of you," "You're doing a great job," or simply "I love you," they may spend their lives chasing validation from others—teachers, peers, romantic partners, and work.

That's why I aim to raise my kids in a home where they never have to guess how I feel about them. I want to be the voice in their heads telling them, "You are capable," "You are kind," and "You are enough." It's not about empty praise or rewarding mediocrity. It's about recognizing their effort, their character, and their unique gifts. It's about showing them that who they are is valued—not just what they achieve.

Compliments don't have to be grand or elaborate. Sometimes, the simplest statements can have the biggest impact. Things such as: "I noticed how hard you worked on that." "You were so kind to your friend today." "You make me laugh every day, and I love that about you." Compliments like these show our kids that we're paying attention to the little things, not just the big milestones.

I also want to teach my children how to compliment themselves. I've noticed that the way I speak to my kids becomes the way they speak to themselves. If we model positive self-talk and encouragement, they'll learn to do the same. On the flip side, if our words are critical or absent, they may internalize that negativity, carrying it with them into adulthood.

Being the first person to compliment your children is more than just vocalizing kind words—it's building their foundation. It's giving them a safe place to land when the world feels harsh and unforgiving. It's planting seeds of confidence and self-love that will grow for a lifetime.

Because if they don't hear it from you, who will they hear it from?

Give your kid(s) a compliment today. A simple "I'm proud of you" will suffice.

23

Don't Let It Slip

The rapper Eminem has been very open about how important it is to him to be a good father to his daughters. He's been candid about his drug addiction and how it negatively affected his family and nearly took his life. "I don't even deserve the father title," he raps in "Somebody Save Me." The song is about what could've happened if he'd let his addiction win, and all the moments he would've missed with his daughters.

I resonate with Eminem's story not just because I love his music (I do), but because I too struggled heavily with drug use, and I too got sober so I wouldn't miss out on my children's lives.

When I was thirteen years old, I started abusing Adderall, nicotine, and beer, and by seventeen, it had turned into a full-blown addiction to opiates, alcohol, and cocaine. By the age of twenty-three, I had friends who died from drug abuse, and after a near overdose myself, I knew I would be right behind them if I kept going at the pace I was. I decided to quit the hard stuff in hopes of stopping the downward spiral of chaos that had become my life. I channeled my addictive personality into fitness and started a business.

By the time I was thirty-one, I was married to the love of my life, we'd bought our first home, and we were about to have our first child. My wife and I were both excited and terrified. To help manage these big emotions, I turned to my coping mechanism: alcohol. The next six years were filled with the absolute best moments of my life, sprinkled with some of the worst, because I had this little devil on my shoulder telling me that four drinks were just an appetizer. The fact that we had our second-born right before the world shut down in 2020 only made things harder, and I gave my early twenties a run for their money in terms of alcohol consumption. I was missing out on my kids' lives. When my desire to be a present dad overcame my desire to cope through alcohol, I got sober from the one substance I still had a problem with, on January 2, 2023.

If there are some addictions ruling your life, be honest with yourself. There's only one thing worse than putting something before your kids and missing out on the moments with them, and that is not apologizing if you did. Capture it; don't let it slip.

What's getting in the way when it comes to being present in your kids' lives? Be honest with yourself.

24

The Everyday Acts of Heroism

Parents often declare, "I would die for my children." It expresses how much we love our children, more than our own lives. We may never have to die for our children, but we most certainly have to live for them.

How are you *living* for them? How's your health? How are your habits? How's your relationship with your partner? How many times did you look each kid in the eyes today? What words did you speak that made them feel good about themselves? These are choices we can make every day. Sure, dying for them is heroic, but you have the opportunity to be their hero every single day. Of course you would lay your life down for theirs, but will you make the necessary changes to *live* for them?

Make a healthy change, no matter how small, as a step toward living for them.

25

Always Pursue Your Children

When I was a teenager, my mom and dad got divorced. I lived with my dad and older brother, and for a while, all three of us were just surviving, trying to navigate our new normal. My dad was busy with work, my brother was often away, and I was left alone a lot, without much guidance. I don't hold this against my dad because we were all going through it, and while I wouldn't say it was the sole reason I turned to drugs and alcohol to help me cope, feeling disconnected from my father together with the ease of turning everything off through substances made the lifestyle appealing.

No matter the age of your children, make it a point to always pursue them. When our children are young, it's easy to spend quality time with them, because at that age, we are their everything. As they get older, they naturally become more independent. We can get comfortable with this new sense of freedom and forget that we still need to pursue them, even if there's pushback.

It's not about forcing time spent together (a tactic that usually fails spectacularly with teenagers); it's about establishing a routine. We have family friends who are now empty nesters. They told me that when their kids were teenagers, they would schedule a family meeting night every week. No matter what was going on or how busy they were, no one could cancel family meeting night. This simple routine maintained their connection. And even though some complaining was inevitable, they never let up. Their relationship with their kids remains strong even with the kids now out of the house, and they still hold family meetings to connect with one another—just less frequently.

The teenage years are challenging, and there will come a day when your child views their friend group the way they once viewed you. There will likely come a day when they create their own life with their own family. But this does not mean you should stop pursuing them. Just because they don't reciprocate your efforts in the same way they used to doesn't mean you should stop the outings, the one-on-one time, or the conversations. Whether or not you feel it in the moment, they still want to be pursued—always and forever.

How can you continue to pursue your kids as they get older? It's never too early to think about this.

26

Embracing the Bittersweet Journey of Parenthood

When my daughter turned seven, she suddenly went from calling our vacation a "buhcation" to pronouncing it correctly. When I heard it, it felt like a blow to the gut, like in one day she had gone from being my baby to being a little kid. One day, we will pick up our children for the last time. We won't know it in the moment—it'll just happen. It can be heartbreaking to realize your child will never be that way again. They will never mispronounce that word in their adorable way again. They will never ask you to tie their shoes, reach their favorite toy on the shelf, or hold their hand in quite the same way.

But this is life. This is part of the journey of parenthood.

And it's also the goal.

As parents, we are tasked with the bittersweet mission of raising our children to one day not need us the same way they do now. The goal isn't to keep them in these precious moments forever, no matter how tempting that may feel. The goal is to watch them grow into independent adults, to stumble and make mistakes, to grow into the humans we've lovingly guided them to be. It's an odd paradox—to cherish every brief glimpse while also preparing to let them each go.

Parenting is full of goodbyes. Every new phase means saying goodbye to the one before it. Yes, it can be heartbreaking. There are days I wish I could hit the pause button, to linger a little longer in my children's laughter, their wide-eyed wonder, or the feeling of their tiny arms wrapped tightly around my neck. Or at least I'd like to pump the brakes, to slow it all down. But it is also achingly beautiful. Because as our children outgrow needing us in the ways they do now, they step into a future where they will need us differently. One day, they won't need us to pick them up physically—but if we build a strong connection now, they will need us more than ever to pick them up emotionally. They will need us for wisdom, guidance, and unconditional love.

For every phase we say goodbye to, we gain the privilege of seeing them step into who they are becoming. We trade the simplicity of now for the complexity of tomorrow, and we get to be there for it all—if we embrace it.

And when the day comes that my children don't need me to pick them up, I'll remind myself that I've prepared for this moment, and I'll be there for the next. Because that's the essence of parenthood: letting go, little by little, while always holding space for them in our hearts.

What's something you can do to hold on to a memory of what your kids are like in this season? Some ideas: keeping a journal of funny things they say, printing pictures, saving videos, or collecting their artwork into a book.

27

Childlike Wisdom

Our children can teach us so much about life if we let them.

My daughter casually said to me that the world is not perfect. "It's almost perfect," she said, "but it's not quite there. It's magical in the way we're able to talk, be born, the way birds fly, but because there's death and bad, bad people in the world, it's not perfect. The perfect place is where we go after we die."

"Why do you think it isn't perfect?" I asked.

"If everyone was perfect, how would we learn? We have to make mistakes to learn."

I would love to take full credit for the powerful words she speaks, but the only thing my wife and I can take credit for is the fact that we encourage her mind. We encourage her to read, to think, to speak, and we ask questions rather than simply respond. I sit back in awe and watch this child of mine speak wisdom.

Sometimes, children have to grow up too quickly. This could be for a number of reasons: bad parenting, the darkness of this world entering their lives too soon, or simply the circumstances they were dealt. If you are fortunate enough to have an innocent child, protect that innocence for as long as possible. Listen to what they have to say about the world. Encourage their imagination, their freethinking, and their questions—even if those questions challenge you.

Listen to your children. Their childlike outlook on the world might be just what we so desperately need to change it.

What has your child taught you or how has their mere existence shaped your outlook on life?

28

My Wife Was Once a Little Girl

A while back, I found a picture of my wife when she was seven years old. I thought it was cute, and so I hung it in my car to make us smile. Over time, especially after we had our daughter, it became something much more meaningful. That picture reminds me that my wife was once a little girl—a little girl who viewed the world with innocence before it revealed its true colors and she was forced to deal with challenges too early.

In a long-term relationship, it's easy to forget where the other person came from. We go about our days, getting so annoyed by socks on the floor, laundry piling up, and the mental load of everyday life, that we forget who the other person *is*. Not just the person we married, but the whole person who existed before we came into the picture. Those little annoyances? Our ego frames them as things happening *to* us. But if we pause, we might see it differently—like how socks on the floor might mean comfort to your partner, a sign of ease in your shared space. Of course, mutual respect and responsibility matter, but grace in marriage should flow abundantly.

That picture of my wife as a little girl urges me to nurture her inner child, to be mindful of her triggers, to understand her past, and to help her heal. It encourages me to offer her the same patience and tenderness I give my daughter. Any girl dad can probably relate: We give our daughters so much grace, maybe to a fault. Our queens deserve it too.

As parents, we all hope our children grow up to have healthy, loving relationships. We hope that the partner who comes into their life sees their worth as we see it, treats them as lovingly as we do. The little girl my wife once was is still inside her, still carrying her hopes, goals, and her view of the world. And now, with my children's little eyes watching me, absorbing every action, deciding what will feel "normal" to them, this is my opportunity to show them everything the little girl inside my wife didn't get to see.

Find a picture of someone in your life you want to have more grace for and put it somewhere you can see every day.

29

Redefining What It Means to Be a Provider

For generations, men were raised to believe that the role of a husband and father is primarily defined by financial provision. Earning a paycheck and putting food on the table was seen as the ultimate marker of success. And while financial stability is important, these days, many men have come to find that it's not the whole picture. Being a provider goes so much deeper.

If the main way we're providing for our family is financially, they may have food to eat, clothes to wear, and maybe even toys and entertainment, but what about emotional security? Children need a dad who listens, who offers comfort when the world feels overwhelming. A father who is emotionally present provides a sense of security that no amount of money can buy. Whether it's talking through a tough day, cheering from the sidelines, or just being a calm and steady presence, these moments create bonds that last a lifetime.

We provide guidance through our actions. Kids are always watching, absorbing how we handle stress, treat others, and navigate life's challenges. A dad who models respect, humility, and perseverance provides invaluable life lessons. How we treat their mothers, how we apologize when we're wrong, and how we bounce back from failure all leave an imprint far deeper than any material gift.

Fathers provide opportunities for growth. This might mean introducing kids to new experiences: teaching them how to cook, ride a bike, or tackle a problem with confidence. It might be about encouraging curiosity or helping them discover their strengths, thereby helping children build independence and self-worth.

Fathers provide emotional and physical safety. Kids thrive when they know their world is secure, when they feel loved and protected. Providing stability means being dependable, showing up even when life gets hard, and creating a home where your family feels safe to be themselves.

So, what are you providing? Is it just a paycheck, or is it the best of yourself? True provision is about so much more than money. It's about giving your family the tools, love, and confidence they need to flourish. The legacy we leave behind won't be measured by what we earned, but by how we loved, taught, and supported the people closest to us.

Reflect on everything you provide as a dad.

30

Small Gestures Create Lifelong Memories

When I was a kid, my dad would wake up early on Saturday mornings to get doughnuts for us. This memory is imprinted in my mind. It was such a simple gesture, but it meant so much to me—that he took the time to give me and my siblings a treat each week.

Now that I'm a dad, I've continued the tradition. Most Saturday mornings, I'll see which of my children is awake—usually both—and then we head to the doughnut shop. There's a peace to the ten-minute car ride: the sunrise, not many cars on the road, my kids still in their pajamas, with messy hair and sleepy breath. These mornings are especially magical on cold winter days.

We enter the shop, which is actually an Airstream trailer, and my children pick out their doughnuts. I order two coffees—strong, with a dash of cream—one for me and one for my wife. My kids usually start eating their doughnuts on the short ride home, but I tell them to wait. When we get home and the kids are at the counter eating their doughnuts, my wife and I sipping our coffees, the dog begging for a taste of a dropped crumb, a Saturday morning cartoon in the background, it creates an imprint of a memory for them. A routine that started in my childhood is one I now hold dear to my heart as a father.

My wife and I have created other traditions, such as family days, usually on Sundays, where we play games, go on hikes, visit a bookstore, or just go exploring. We also have a family dinner night, where we cook together or, at the very least, eat together at the table. We try to do this every night, but realistically it's about four nights a week. Baking cookies, making hot chocolate, roasting marshmallows—the list goes on—are all little gestures that we do so often they've become traditions. Just as I am continuing doughnut Saturdays from my childhood, I hope my kids bring these little traditions into their adulthood.

Kids care about the small gestures the most—the ones that don't cost a lot of money, the ones that don't take up a lot of time, but the ones that are consistent and show them you were thinking about them. The ones that show you cared enough to do this for them.

Create a small gesture that can become a small tradition. Feel free to include doughnut Saturdays in your family routine!

31

First-Time Parents, First-Time Healing

If you experienced pain and trauma in your childhood, how have you taken that with you into your parenting?

In *Good Will Hunting,* there's a scene where Sean (Robin Williams) sits with Will (Matt Damon) and repeatedly tells him, "It's not your fault." At first, Will brushes it off with a nod, assuming it's just a platitude. But Sean doesn't stop. He keeps saying it until Will finally hears it—until it sinks in. It's not just a moment of catharsis for Will, it's a challenge. It's an invitation to let go of the idea that his pain and trauma define him. That scene reminds us that while we're not to blame for the harm done to us, we *are* responsible for deciding what happens next. Do we let our trauma consume us? Or do we stop the wave of pain before it crashes into another generation?

We might blame our shortcomings on our parents' flaws, carrying resentment for the way they parented instead of focusing on how we're choosing to parent today. Dwelling on their mistakes doesn't fix ours. It only keeps us tethered to the past.

Whatever happened in the past, you have the power to put up the dam that stops that wave from getting your children wet. That's how you break any curse, that's how you, as a first-time parent, heal the trauma that affected you.

There's a first time for everything, and our children deserve to be the first to experience a childhood marked by your love, rather than your trauma.

I really hope you've seen* Good Will Hunting. *You know what to do if you haven't. What are you doing with your children to break the cycles from the past? Reflect on this today.

32

The Comparison Trap

It's easy to get caught in the comparison trap. We compare ourselves to other parents, to our peers, and even to our own parents. Some of us strive to become the parent we always wanted for ourselves. Others measure their worth against the father down the street, the business owner on social media, or the friends who seem to have it all figured out. No matter which version of comparison you fall into, it's a trap—a trap that steals joy and leaves behind unhappiness, jealousy, and resentment.

The truth is that comparison often paints a distorted picture. When we compare ourselves to others, we tend to focus on their highlights while magnifying our own shortcomings. We might find ourselves thinking, *Why does their life seem so easy? Why don't I have what they have?* That small, bitter phrase *Must be nice,* creeps in, and suddenly we're spiraling into a cynical mindset.

The danger of this trap is that it drains us of the joy we should be pouring into our children. Our time, energy, and attention are limited, and when we waste them comparing ourselves to others, we have less to give to the people who need us most. The resentment, the regret, the self-doubt—none of it belongs in a father's life. It's noise. And if we're not careful, it becomes the soundtrack playing in the background of our parenthood.

But comparison isn't always external. Sometimes, we look inward, measuring ourselves against the standards set by our own parents. For some, this kind of comparison inspires growth—an opportunity to build on the good and leave behind the bad. Keep the silly dad jokes and shed the harsh words. We can give our kids the freedom we never had or the structure we always craved. In these moments, comparison can be healthy if it fuels self-awareness and improvement.

The world is filled with opportunities for comparison. Social media gives us a curated view of everyone else's success while obscuring the struggles that lie behind the scenes. The only way to keep our joy intact as fathers is to reject the comparison trap altogether.

Celebrate others' successes without letting them diminish your own. Remind yourself that you're on your own path and that your worth isn't tied to someone else's journey. Instead of asking, "Why do they have it better?," ask yourself, "Am I heading in the direction I want to go?"

If the answer is yes, then keep moving forward with confidence. If the answer is no, use that realization as a guide—not to compare yourself to others, but to realign with your own values and goals.

As fathers, our energy is precious. Let's spend it wisely—on building, growing, and showing up, not on measuring ourselves against others. Because at the end of the day, the only comparison worth making is the one between who we are today and who we were yesterday.

Take a moment to celebrate yourself. Write down a few things you're proud of achieving or overcoming recently. No matter how small, these victories demonstrate the progress you're making on your unique path, not anyone else's.

33

A World Full of Distractions

As a social media creator, I have a love/hate relationship with my phone. If I'm honest, the pendulum often swings more toward hate. I'll go on my phone to do a minor task and somehow, thirty minutes later, I'm down a rabbit hole of information I never asked for, wanted, or intended to find. Here I am, distracted by a device created in 2007, which I never predicted would become one of my most common addictions a couple of decades later. The worst is when I catch myself telling my children that I'll play with them, only to get lost in my phone, or feeling the knife twist in my chest when my child says, "Dad, why are you always on your phone?" Hate. Hate. Hate.

But we always have a choice. Even for me, whose livelihood comes from making content that I share online, and that I want others to consume, I can choose to find times to turn off social media, put down the phone, and engage with those around me. I take phone-free weekends where I put my phone away in my room and only check once or twice a day for any important missed calls or texts. I'll also set a nighttime mode or sign off at a certain time to help me engage with my family at the end of the day.

Ferris Bueller had it right: "Life moves pretty fast. If you don't stop and look around once in a while, you could miss it." (And this was in the days before smartphones!) There is always something to be distracted by. What will you do to make sure you're not missing life by scrolling through it?

What are you most distracted by? Develop a plan to limit the distractions to a certain time of the day.

34

Balancing Love Between Children

My wife and I initially planned to have our second child two years after our first. Unfortunately, we had a miscarriage that prevented this. It then turned into three years after our first that my amazing son was born. While people often talk about the overwhelming love you have for each of your children when they're born, many people do not talk about the overwhelming fear that coincides with it.

One of the primary ways this fear manifested for me was worrying that my daughter wouldn't feel love from her mom and me in the same way she had during those first three years when she had our full attention. The love absolutely doubles in size, but a newborn takes up a lot of time, energy, and stress, while a three-year-old wants nothing but your attention. How would we balance this? There was no definitive answer other than the same answer we'd arrived at when we had our first: We'd figure it out.

I doubt I'm the only one who has felt this fear. Worrying about distributing the love evenly comes simply because you love your children with the same magnitude. You want them to feel that love, but our brains, our hormones, and our exhaustion can tell us some really scary stuff. Even our kids sometimes vocalize our worst fears, saying things like "You love him more!," or sometimes even "You don't love me!," and the worst "I hate you!" But it's not true. You're not alone in these feelings or thoughts. Actually, you're among a high class of good parents that truly care. You're doing great.

Do you relate to the sentiments expressed in this chapter? Check on your partner during this time and check on yourself. I promise you, it gets better.

35

The Power of a Bedtime Story

As parents, by the time we get to bedtime, we are as exhausted as our kids! We often don't have the energy required to give more of our attention to a drawn-out bedtime routine. But I've found that when I push through this feeling, I experience something special.

My son's favorite books are *Little Blue Truck*, anything about excavators, and Dr. Seuss. My daughter loved being read to, but in kindergarten she learned to read on her own, and our bedtime routine now looks like reading books next to each other. We try to do this most nights for thirty minutes. My favorite part is when she turns to me and says, "All finished!" I ask her to tell me about what she read, and I find she has turned into a full-blown book critic!

This time together at bedtime is powerful. My children

and I can cry together, laugh together, ponder together, and share thoughts that might not have come up otherwise—all thanks to the bedtime story.

The bedtime story is more than just a routine; it's an imprinted moment. Something that happens so often, our kids can't help but remember it. They'll think about it when they're older and possibly share the same tradition with their own children, just like in the classic children's book *Love You Forever* by Robert Munsch, another good story to read together with your kids (although this one completely wrecked me on multiple occasions).

Read to your children. Read with your children. Set a goal of a certain number of nights per week to read together.

36

Holiday Magic

When my wife and I bought our first home (before we had kids) we went to the store to buy holiday lights. Sticker shock prevented that from happening. Instead, we saw a little lawn ornament that was maybe $25. We bought it, even though it felt like a splurge since it was a want, not a need. We still have it, a penguin with a Santa hat that lights up that we named Pengee. These days, of course, our children love it. We also have a lot of lights on the house now, but that little $25 Pengee is still our most adored decoration.

I absolutely love creating an amazing holiday season for my little humans. I love watching the wild dance my kids do when they realize they got the big gift that was on their list—the one gift they didn't think they'd get.

I love giving my family gifts, but even more I love

teaching the importance of giving, the gratitude that comes with receiving, and cherishing this brief moment in time when magic feels real. My wife and I added a tradition of giving presents to a family in need. It's a simple act, but it reminds us of how fortunate we are and how much of a difference we can make for someone else. Whether it's a gift for someone else or a $25 light-up penguin, sometimes we all can use a reminder that holiday magic doesn't come from expensive decorations or getting the best gift from Santa, it comes from appreciating what is most valuable in your life.

This holiday season, find an opportunity to show your kids how magic comes not just from giving presents but also from giving back.

37

Be Weird

Everyone is weird. Weirdness is just the part of you that views the world differently. To society, being weird is impolite, immature, abnormal, uncomfortable, and outside the lines. The rules don't support weirdness. But if we lose our weirdness, we lose a vital part of what makes us alive. Without weirdness, art wouldn't exist. Technology wouldn't exist. Progress wouldn't happen. Why? Because we'd never answer the questions we're too afraid to ask. We'd never know if we were right because we were too scared of being wrong. We want to fit in. We want to be accepted.

My wife does this weird little dance when she's happy. When we get good news or something exciting happens, she breaks into a little shuffle. I absolutely love it. I see the freedom in her eyes and the joy in her smile. When you can be so freely weird with someone, you know they bring out the best in you, which, when you think about it, is just another way of saying "bringing out the weird in you."

When a child feels comfortable, you'll notice they act "weird." You might have heard a parent say, "Oh, they're not shy—they're just nervous." Once that child feels comfortable, they start acting like their wonderfully weird selves.

I always tell my kids that being called weird is a compliment. It might get harder to prove my case as they grow older, but I hope the message sticks. Weirdness is a lens through which we see the world, and I believe it's the only way to see beyond the ordinary. It's how we see the outer layers, past the normalcy we're told to focus on.

Be weird.

To encourage the weirdness in your family, play charades, share a story, or create a brand-new game where you can all comfortably be your weird selves!

38

The Sweet Spot Where Ambition Meets Presence

When you start a family, life takes on a strange new rhythm. The days stretch longer, but the years feel shorter. It's like sitting in a chair while a treadmill screams beneath you. You went from rushing toward the next phase to being forced to slow down—because now you have a tiny human who doesn't sleep in the middle of the night, who needs you in ways you didn't even know you could be needed.

Time becomes a blur of early mornings, packed lunches, and bedtime stories. But amidst the chaos, something else starts to happen. You begin to wonder about what's next. You look ahead—dreaming, planning, maybe even longing. Where will life take us next? Where will they go to college? Should I start a business? Find a new job? Be busier? Do more?

It's the tension of two worlds colliding: the present you're living and the future you're chasing. It's hard to reconcile both. On one hand, you want to be ambitious—to keep climbing, to provide a better life. On the other hand, you don't want to look up one day and realize you were so focused on what's next that you missed what's now.

I don't think the answer is to give up one for the other. Life isn't that simple. We need ambition—it drives us, gives us purpose, and inspires our children. But ambition without presence? That's where we risk losing ourselves and the moments that matter most.

It's not realistic to stop dreaming about the future. It's also not realistic to expect every mundane moment to feel magical. But maybe it's not about choosing one over the other. Maybe it's about learning to move forward while still noticing the scenery.

The bright red leaf your child picks up during a walk, the slow mornings spent cooking pancakes, the quiet moments of connection—these aren't detours. They're part of the journey. They remind us that we don't have to sacrifice today to build tomorrow.

One day, you'll look back and realize that the life you built and the memories you made weren't separate chapters. They were the same story.

This is your "go touch some grass" moment. Leave your phone at home and take a walk, a run, a cold plunge, or lie on the ground outside. Do something out of your normal routine; take a deep breath and enjoy.

39

Get Up, Stand Up

In fifth grade I went on a field trip with my class. A few of us were playing a game when things got rowdy, and a student who was autistic became the target of teasing from someone in our group. The worst part? The rest of us did nothing about it. We stood there, frozen. A few even laughed. And me? I just watched. I always knew this student was different from me. I never teased or tormented them outright—but does that make it better?

When the teacher noticed and tried to find out who was responsible, my friends and I pleaded that we weren't directly involved. Looking back, I know that standing by in silence was just as wrong as actively participating. That day still haunts me and I am ashamed. I knew better, but I wasn't brave enough to do better.

Now, as a parent, I've made it my mission to teach my

kids about bullying, about the importance of standing up for others, and about doing what's right—no matter what the group is doing. I remind them constantly: *Never let someone diminish someone else.* Stand up. Speak out. Fight back—not always literally, though sometimes even that's necessary. These lessons are personal to me because of what I failed to do as a kid. There will always be bullies, and there will always be those who have no one to stand up for them. But the more we emphasize kindness, courage, and empathy to our children, the less this will happen.

As Dr. Martin Luther King Jr. once said: "In the end, we will remember not the words of our enemies, but the silence of our friends."

Take some time today to talk to your children about standing up for what's right, even when it's difficult.

40

Happy Wife, Happy Life

As long as your wife is happy, you're happy, right? Wrong.

This saying can be misunderstood to mean that you should make your wife happy at the expense of your own well-being. And that, inevitably, leads to resentment and burnout. I've seen people endure this imbalance for years—on both sides. What this creates isn't a marriage; it's a one-sided relationship.

A few years ago, I learned that Slipknot was coming to town. They were a bucket list band I really wanted to see. The show included an option for a package where fans could see a backstage exhibit showing the evolution of the infamous masks, outfits, and other fun (and okay, nerdy) metalhead stuff. I wanted to go but didn't know how I could justify spending the money or leaving my wife to hold down the fort for the night for something as frivolous as a concert. But when I brought it up to her, she said without hesitation, "Go!"

I realized that in my quest to be the best husband and dad, I never thought about taking a step back to just be me. To let loose, to relax, to replenish. In that moment, my wife knew more than I did that I needed to do something I was interested in, for my well-being. Maybe it meant a slight inconvenience for her, but she showed me how marriage isn't about sacrificing yourself to keep someone else smiling. It's about building a partnership where you both work to bring out the best in each other.

And I'm happy to report that the Slipknot concert was one of the best heavy metal concerts I've ever been to.

Surprise your partner with something that will bring a smile to their face.

41

Let Them Struggle

"I'm not like other kids, Dad," my daughter said to me one evening.

"What do you mean, sweetie?" I asked, nervous to hear her response.

"I'm scared of movies my friends like. I'm scared of the dark. I like to eat seaweed for a snack, and kids make fun of me for it. And I don't think I'm brave. I'm just so different."

Hearing my precious daughter struggle with feeling different from all her friends, and how they were responding to her, was tough. My first thought was *How do I fix this? How do I stop the struggle?* I took a breath and instead listed all the things that make her unique, the things that make her brave, and the qualities that make her who she is. I reiterated that it doesn't matter what other people think, what matters is that we are true to ourselves.

A week later, she told me about a different experience at school. She shared how she had stood up to a classmate who wasn't being very nice to her. She'd said, "I don't care what you have to say about me. My dad says we don't care what others think."

My heart swelled with pride.

I've lived long enough to understand that struggle is mandatory—for life and for growth. The best parts of life are often on the other side of struggle. Still, I wish there were a way my kids didn't have to struggle. A part of me believes I could take on their struggles for them. That part of me is the love I have for my children. But the other part of my love knows better. It knows that because I love them, I need to let them struggle. I need to guide them through it, give them the tools I believe will help, and be there for them when it feels like too much.

When those struggles come, they'll turn to us—the superheroes who can make it all better. And, sometimes, we will have the power to fix things. But should we? If we do, they might not develop the skills to handle it when it happens again. They need to learn. They need to struggle before the safety net that we as parents provide is gone and it's too late.

I'm learning every day. I'm making a game plan for the future, for when my kids are older. Sometimes I will make my own mistakes. Sometimes I will need to listen instead of fix. Sometimes I will need to ask, *What will prevent them from getting hurt later?* Sometimes, the answer is struggle. That's the irony: While they're struggling, so am I.

There will be mistakes. There will be struggle. And there will be lessons learned. That, too, is essential for living.

How can you safely let your kids struggle today? An easy example: I let my daughter get ready for school without any help from her mom or me. If she's late for the bus, there's a consequence.

42

I Love You

At the end of the day, I often reflect on how many times I've said *I love you* to my wife and children. And I mean it every time. In fact, whenever I exchange *I love you* with my wife, I stop and say, "No, you don't understand. *I love you.*" These three words aren't enough to encompass the depth of my feelings. Love is more than an emotion—it's an experience. I'll repeat it, sometimes five or more times, until she blushes. That's when I know she feels it, that she knows I truly mean it.

I don't think it's possible to say *I love you* too much. There are times when I'm in the car, and I glance in the rearview mirror to tell my child or children in the back-seat, "I love you." They'll respond with the same words—unless they're taking a nap. It's customary to say these three words when we leave the house or end a conversation, but those moments are expected. It's the random moments that matter most. In the middle of morning chaos and hustle, a spontaneous *I love you* has the power to relax the shoulders, open the lungs for a deep breath, ease the soul, and reassure everyone under this roof that they are loved. It's a reset.

What this habit has done is remarkable—it's already been passed on. I catch my son randomly telling me, his mom, and his sister the magical three words. Everyone in the house has picked up on the habit. Those words may never fully capture the weight of the emotion behind them, but they are never used loosely in our home. They're said often—yet still, never enough. If I were to calculate how many *I love you*s a day would equal how much I actually love them, the answer would be infinite.

Today, set a record with the number of times you say "I love you." Say it genuinely, with eye contact, or follow it up with a hug.

43

The Value of a Dollar

How we were raised often greatly impacts how we want our children to approach the topic of money. If you grew up without much money, you probably want to give your children far more than you had. If you came from nothing and built your success from the ground up, you might want your children to work for their success in the same way, with your guidance. You might struggle with a scarcity mindset and unintentionally pass that along.

On the flip side, if you grew up with money, you may take a more structured approach. You may naturally pass on that generational wealth and spend your money freely (perhaps overly so, at times). Or maybe you grew up seeing the dark side of wealth—greed, overwork, workaholism—and chose instead to live a simpler, more frugal life.

No matter our situation, money becomes complicated once we have a family of our own.

My father used to tell me, "You need to know the value of a dollar." It usually came in response to me asking for something he wouldn't buy, and I'd stomp off, annoyed. When I turned sixteen, I got my first real job at the local pizza joint. Working hard to earn money, I slowly began to understand what my dad had been telling me about the value of a dollar. Ever since then, I've worked hard, both at jobs I enjoyed and at jobs that bored me to death. Each of these jobs taught me something important about the value of money that I now try to pass along to my kids, even at a young age.

I'll be honest—I love buying my children the things that they want. I want to provide them with opportunities, and sometimes those opportunities come with a price tag. I don't think there's anything wrong with that, as long as I don't lose sight of teaching them the value of money and dedicated work. Saving my entire paycheck for their future schooling, programs, or their first house feels like a disservice. I understand the instinct, but I don't want to miss an opportunity to show them what it takes to earn and build something for themselves.

I want to guide my kids from the sidelines and see what they can create on their own. What if they achieve things far beyond what we ever did? How will we know if we don't put them in the driver's seat? We can talk to them about these lessons, but we know life experience goes so much further.

Warren Buffet once said in an interview that he would provide his children "enough [money] so that they can do anything, but not so much that they can do nothing." I love the mentality of giving them enough, but not enough to do nothing. Warren Buffett's definition of *enough* is probably very different from mine, but the message resonates. However I choose to help my children financially, I hope it leaves room for them to explore, learn, and understand the value of how they got there.

If your children are old enough to earn money or learn about money, what can you do to teach them the value of a dollar?

44

The Patient Parent

Patience is the companion of wisdom.
—SAINT AUGUSTINE

"My patience is running thin." "You're really testing my patience right now." I know I'm not the only parent who has said—or at least thought—these things! Children test our patience daily. They desperately (and constantly) want our attention, and we desperately (and often) want to be alone, and the tension between those two leads to impatience and inner turmoil.

With patience comes inner peace. The kind of peace you find when you let go of the messy house, the endless to-do list, the terrible phone call with your boss, the child repeatedly asking for a snack, and all those stressful adult responsibilities that rob us of our calm.

We live in a non-peaceful world and an impatient

society. If you can find patience in parenting, you can find patience anywhere. It's the ultimate test, and how often you're tested depends on how much time you spend with your children.

Whether or not I respond to a request with patience will make a lasting impact on a temporary situation. The situation won't last forever, but how we respond might.

How's your patience these days? Is there some external factor that you can limit that might reduce your stress? Reflect on this today and work on letting it go.

45

Effort Over Results

The journey is the reward.
—Chinese proverb

Riding a bike is one of the first lessons that taught me how life is a journey of falling and getting back up again. I don't remember how long it took me to learn, or the perseverance it required, but I do remember when my dad and brother pushed me off on the bike and I soared down the hill and into a new life of freedom. The triumph, the feeling of accomplishment—now I could ride with my older brother, I could get a milkshake nearby—was unforgettable.

I may not remember it, but I'm sure there were plenty of times I fell off the bike as I learned to ride. In life, the stakes can be high. But in childhood, there are safe ways to learn the value of effort, risk, and even failure. It's not ease that makes the journey worthwhile, it's the training, the practice, and the effort that produce results. Not perfect, flawless results every time, but the kind of growth that comes from trying. This is what I want my children to understand: I'm not overly concerned with the results. I care about the effort—that they didn't quit. They won't become the best at everything, and that's okay. What matters is that they keep trying, because effort and resilience will carry them further than talent alone.

I want to teach them that hard workers never quit, and that growth comes from the journey, regardless of the outcome. If the outcome doesn't go the way they want, that's when we need to show up, help our kids get back up, and, most importantly, resist the urge to push the bike up the mountain for them.

Instead, we steady their handlebars and watch them ride off again.

Eventually, they will soar down the hill. And when they land, they'll know that it wasn't just about reaching the bottom, it was about the strength they built along the way.

We have a rule in our house that when it comes to commitments, like playing a sport, if you sign up, you finish. You don't have to sign up again, but there is no quitting midseason. Is there a similar rule you could use to help your kids understand that what matters is the effort, not the results?

46

Uncomfortable Conversations

You probably remember "the talk"—maybe you called it "the birds and the bees." I distinctly remember beating my dad to the punch in sixth grade when I came home asking what "sixty-nine" meant. He froze. Now that I'm a dad, I don't blame him! This and other conversations about uncomfortable topics feel awkward. But despite my discomfort, I want my kids to feel comfortable asking questions about anything, knowing they won't face judgment. If they don't feel safe asking me, they'll find their answers somewhere else—and I might not like what they find.

Recently, I shared a funny story with another parent about something reckless I did as a teenager involving alcohol. Instead of laughing, they looked nervous, glancing around to make sure their teenager wasn't nearby to hear. The reason I'm open with my kids about my mistakes is because I believe they shaped me, and that sharing these stories, uncomfortable as it may be, gives my kids something valuable: context.

When I was younger, I craved raw emotion from my parents. I wanted their stories to guide my path. Instead, I had to find my own answers. When we're open with our kids, we're more than just authority figures saying "Don't do that." We show them the "why" behind the rules, helping them navigate their own decisions with clarity.

I know my children will probably read this book one day. They'll see the good, the bad, and the deeply uncomfortable. And I'm okay with that because I want them to understand me, not just as their dad but as a person who's lived, made mistakes, and grown. You might choose to keep certain things private, and that's fine. But your story—your willingness to have difficult conversations—can provide direction. You might help your child avoid a misstep or find a better way forward. When we hide who we were, we rob them of the chance to become who they're meant to be.

How comfortable are you with the uncomfortable topics? Do you have an idea about the approach you will take? Reflect on this now so that you're ready when your kid comes to you with a question.

47

A Job Well Done

I've played the tape forward more times than I can count. The tape of my life as a father. Where will I mess up? What will I regret? Did I prepare them enough? Did I instill what I wanted to? Was I the example they needed? Did I live by my word? And will I feel like I did a good job in the end?

What will your kids bring up later in life when they describe what you were like as a dad? I think my kids will remember how I liked things organized and clean. I also think they will remember how much I loved them, cared for them, spent quality time with them, and showed up to every activity. This makes me feel like I'm doing a lot right, like I'm putting in the effort now that will hopefully make them look back on their childhoods as ones marked by love, fun, and support. It's too early to say for sure. I hope they'll say that I was always there for them. I always had their back. I always had the conversations. I always knew the right thing to say at the right time.

One day, your children will understand you weren't perfect. They'll understand *they* weren't perfect. They may understand why you are the way you are. They will understand what you did for them. Sure, they may remember the gifts and the financial support, but the long-lasting effects are the memories of time spent together. The way you talked to them, cared for them, laughed with them, and lit up the room with your smile every time they walked in.

Dads, we will never stop showing up. We have made mistakes, but we never quit. We didn't just do our best—we did more than that. We are doing more than that. We are breaking the curses like never before—not just one of them, all of them. We are paving our own path.

We're not done yet because we are never done. We're in this until our card is pulled. This job is never done.

How do you think your kids will describe you as a father later in life? How does that make you feel? If you don't feel like it describes "a job well done," reflect on how you might do things differently.

48

Lighting Up the Room

Whenever I meet a parent who has a great relationship with their grown kids, I always ask what they did to build that connection. I recently posed this question to the mother of our family's babysitter. This young woman has been our family's babysitter for most of our children's lives, and we've had the honor of watching her grow from a teenager into an amazing adult. Seeing the way our children adore her, I know that her parents did something right in how they raised her, and so I was curious to hear what she'd say.

The answer stayed with me: "Every time one of my kids enters the room, I greet them with a smile. Not just any smile, but a smile that shows excitement that they're here. A smile that lights up the room." What an incredible habit.

I now make it a point to smile at my kids every time they enter a room or come home. Greeted like this, with admiration and love, they feel how important they are to you. Even if they've only been gone for a few hours, they know they were missed by the way you react to their presence.

Everyone loves the feeling of genuine appreciation—of being noticed and cared about. Think about how good it feels when a friend smiles as you enter a room. Your kids lit up the room the second they were born; let them feel that same light every time they walk into one.

Make a point to smile at your kids when they walk into the room today. See if you notice a change in the energy of your home.

49

Let Them Fly

In the movie *Dead Poets Society,* Neil Perry is a teenager whose father, Mr. Perry, pressures him to pursue a career in medicine, even though Neil is passionate about acting and dreams of being onstage. This conflict between parental expectations and individual desires is central to Neil's storyline and ultimately leads to a tragic outcome.

When we have children, it's normal to have dreams about what they will grow up to be. Sometimes we want them to become what we always wanted to be. We anticipate that athletic scholarship, or that they'll become the valedictorian, the actor, the doctor, the writer, or whatever hopes we may have had for ourselves. If we're really fortunate, they might even become what we envisioned. These dreams are harmless if they are expressed lightly, so that our children won't feel the pressure or fear of disappointing us.

It becomes a problem when we put pressure on our children to achieve the things we wanted but never accomplished. They aren't here to fill that void. Do you know what I think is the most beautiful thing? Seeing my children find their own passions and talents. My wife and I can influence them by introducing them to music, art, sports, or anything else we want. But watching them discover—or maybe even choose—the things we've shown them is like watching them grow wings and fly into the sunset. To witness them find something in life that lights them up, that gives them identity and purpose, is a privilege beyond words.

Mr. Perry was a father who never dealt with the emptiness in his soul or took the time to notice how happy his son was when he rebelliously took part in *A Midsummer Night's Dream*. In contrast, the protagonist of the story, Robin Williams's iconic character English teacher Mr. Keating, serves as the real father figure. As he says to his students early in the film, "Carpe diem. Seize the day, boys. Make your lives extraordinary."

As parents, our role is to show our children how to grow wings, how to care for them, how to dry them off when they get wet, how to repair them when they get torn, how to heal them when they get bruised, and, eventually, how to fly. Watching our children soar is one of life's greatest gifts.

Are you letting your kids fly or clipping their wings?

50

The Family Dinner Table

Before my parents' divorce, our family of five met together each evening at the dinner table. Mom cooked (Please don't be pot roast! Does anyone else despise the smell and taste of pot roast? I digress.), and then we'd sit down to share the meal along with stories of our days.

Being the youngest, I was the amusing one. My stories consisted of who was a bully on the tetherball court, how I liked a girl but she hated me, and the best one: how I did something better than my older brother could do it. A slug to the arm, followed by my mother giving my brother a light slug to the arm, was always in the forecast.

My mother would complain about a co-worker or share good news about family plans that would require a shopping trip. My father, stressed about my mom's shopping after seeing bills that could fill a filing cabinet, spoke few words. Instead, he asked questions, more concerned with our lives than his own. His face, however, signified that a storm was brewing.

Then it all stopped. I was young when our dinners together at the table disappeared, but looking back, I realize that it was probably a good indicator that there was turmoil in my family. Dinner became pizza or even cereal. Sometimes Mom wasn't home, and Dad went to bed without eating. My sister got married, moved out, and my older brother was out late with friends, girlfriends, who knows? What I do know is that I was finally able to watch *The Simpsons* without anyone saying, "Turn that off—it's dinnertime!" I'll never forget the emptiness I felt when the family dinners ended.

Now that I am a dad, I have made it a point to bring back the family dinner. I look forward to watching my children grow at the table. To the stories they'll tell us, their new interests, and the bond that will grow between us all. And by bringing my family back to the dinner table, I hope it will inspire my children to do the same with their families someday.

The dinner table is a place for genuine human connection that endures for generations. A place where dreams are born. A place where families are forever united. A place of comfort.

How many nights a week are you able to sit together at the dinner table? This week, try to sit together each night with no distractions and see what stories emerge.

51

The Transformative Power of Parenthood

Jerry Seinfeld shared something the legendary actor Warren Beatty once told him: "One of the nice things God does is that He doesn't let people who don't have kids know what they're missing." Warren, who was fifty-four when he had his first child, had already lived an extraordinary life—one filled with money, fame, women, and success. He seemingly had it all. But when Jerry visited his home, he saw something that shifted his perspective. Warren's once-pristine office was now scattered with toys. At the time, Jerry didn't have children and didn't fully understand it. But the way fatherhood had clearly transformed Warren made it intriguing: A man who had "everything" before he had kids now realized he'd been missing out on something far more meaningful.

Growing up, I always wanted to be a dad. Just as some little girls fantasize about their wedding day, I envisioned what fatherhood might look like. I imagined a house filled with warmth, holidays brimming with magic, and family road trips full of laughter.

Still, I couldn't have understood how completely my life would change until my first child was born. That's when I realized that this life that just came into the world was now a more important extension of my own. I always thought that my role as a father would be to teach my children how the world works. In reality, my children are often the ones teaching me. Lessons in how to be genuine, how to be patient, how to be loving, how to be vulnerable, how to be present, and so much more.

Warren Beatty was right: You don't know the feeling of having your own children until you have them. You don't know if you can handle it until you're in it. Every day, I'm reminded of how radically my children have changed me. I didn't know what I was missing before—but now I do. That realization grounds me in gratitude and keeps my perspective where it belongs.

You are allowed to be both the teacher and the student. Some of your greatest lessons will come from the child you are raising.

How has fatherhood changed your life?

52

Circles of LOVE

"If you draw a circle and keep going around it, even after I die, that's how much I love you." These words from my eight-year-old as I tucked her into bed stopped me in my tracks. I had to write them down, ensuring they'd never fade from my memory. Over the years, there have been countless times she's said, "You're the best dad," or simply, "I love you, Daddy." These words never get old. But sometimes, kids say the most beautiful things at precisely the moment you need them most.

There have been times when I've come home from a long, hard day and feel like I'm failing. Regrets from the past resurface and self-doubt creeps in. Then, just as I'm teetering on the edge of self-sabotage, something marvelous happens. My child will wrap their little arms around me and say, "You're the best daddy in the world." Those simple words, that pure appreciation, can save me. They pull me back from the brink and remind me of who I am and what matters most.

I often wonder if children have an intuition we sometimes miss as adults. It's easy to overlook their ability to sense when we need their love the most, as if they can see right into our hearts and know the exact moment we're struggling. Their love is so pure, so unfiltered, that it brings me to my knees. I wish I could bottle it up and keep it as medicine for the harder days.

Moments like these ground us. They force us to pause, to see the immense love we have right in front of us, and to understand its true richness. These affirmations from our children aren't coincidences; they're signs. Signs to keep going, to persevere, to never give up on ourselves. Life will, without fail, get hard. Doubt will creep in, jobs will drain us, and external pressures will mount. But the infinite love we share with our children and partners is our constant. It's our lifeline.

That circle my daughter described feels like more than just a metaphor for her love—it's a reminder of the unbreakable bond we share. I imagine it as a pulsating electric force, sparking to life every time we choose love, every time we keep going despite the hard days. It grows brighter and larger each time we express that love to others, each time we let it pull us back from the brink. It's a reminder that even in the darkest moments, we're connected by something bigger than ourselves.

When life feels overwhelming, hold on to that circle. Picture it glowing brighter with every hug, every laugh, and every moment of perseverance. Let it remind you that you are enough, that love surrounds you, and that the life you're building is worth every ounce of effort. Keep going, keep loving, and keep growing that circle—it's the most important work you'll ever do.

Today we're not going to let negative thoughts about ourselves fill our brains. Think instead about a positive affirmation or remember something your children have said. We're digging ourselves out.

53

Who Cares if It Doesn't Match?

One morning, my daughter came downstairs before school wearing my wife's old tap dance recital outfit. Crafted circa 1993, this dress had all the sequins, bright colors, and showmanship characteristic of the era. It even had musical notes sewn into the bright red fabric. Mind you, my daughter was in second grade, and it wasn't costume or dress-up day—at least not for the other students. My daughter was so proud of her outfit that I knew if I reacted negatively, it would've crushed her.

The first thing I asked was "What's today?" She usually chooses her outfits based on a theme: something she watched, a subject they're learning about, or a doll she has. "I have music class today," she replied. I nodded. "That makes sense."

Maybe it's my punk rock upbringing or the fact that I grew up watching MTV red carpets, but I hate dress codes. What's "presentable"? I'll be the judge of how I want to present myself, thank you very much. Style is creative expression, not to mention, it's fun. Yeah, maybe it doesn't match, but it matches who I am today.

Allowing my kids to choose their own outfits is more than just a fun activity; to me it's a vital part of their development. It teaches them to make decisions, stand by their choices, and understand that it's okay to be different. I want to encourage creativity in their minds, and every mismatched outfit is a lesson in creativity and self-confidence.

As a parent, my job isn't to mold my kids into a perfect image but to let them discover who they are—and to celebrate that discovery every single day. So, no, wearing the pirate eye patch with a tutu doesn't match, but in this family, we match our clothes to our personalities, and that's the best match of all.

Pick a day and let your kids wear whatever they want. Better yet, have everyone in the family dress in their "most creative" outfits and go see a movie. Make it a tradition!

54

Be Your Word

Growing up, my dad would always tell me, "If you say you're going to do something, do it. If you say you're going to be somewhere, be there early." My dad is a man of his word. He practiced what he preached, and I can't say there has ever been a time when, if he said he was going to do something, he didn't do it.

A few weeks ago, I told my daughter—no, I promised her—that I was going to take her somewhere. And then I got busy. I was speeding downhill on a mountain of productivity, unstoppable. That is, until my daughter asked me when we were going to fulfill that promise. I told her I was in the middle of something. Her response gutted me: "Daddy, you said we don't break promises." Seeing the disappointment in her eyes, the tears forming, caused me to crash the bike

I had been riding down the mountain of hyperproductivity headfirst into a boulder with no helmet on.

I stopped what I was doing and responded, "You're right." This wasn't about money; it was about my word. My daughter was holding me to my word. She had placed every fiber of her trust into that promise and I broke it, along with the glowing organ in her chest. Cue childhood movie trauma. (*E.T.*, for all of you wondering.) If I had given her a $100 bill at that moment or said, "Let me just hop on Amazon and buy you a Barbie," it wouldn't have compared to the joy that lit up her face when I kept my promise. She reminded me how important it is to do something when you say you're going to do it. Being a man of your word is far more valuable than money.

Do you feel like your follow-through game is on point?

55

You're Not Superman . . . and That's Okay

We all want to be Superman to our kids, but maturing as a father means showing them that we're not.

I will never forget the night my dad told me that he and my mother were getting a divorce. I was fourteen years old. He stood there, bags under his eyes, hair messy, and in a low, defeated voice said, "Your mom and I are filing for divorce. We will do our best to continue to raise you together." I wasn't surprised by the divorce as much as I was surprised by how worn down my father was in that moment. This was a man who had enlisted in the U.S. Marine Corps during the Vietnam War at the ripe age of seventeen. A man who had slept in mud in the middle of a jungle, not knowing if he'd wake up to see tomorrow, now stood in the middle of his bedroom, broken down from life. He had always been my hero, but in this moment, he was also human.

Seeing my dad as human, watching him overcome struggles and become a better dad afterward, made my appreciation for him run deeper. It taught me resilience, empathy, and made me wear my crown of fatherhood with pride. A father isn't a child's hero because he's perfect. A father is a child's hero because of his love and his determination to follow through no matter what life brings. My dad revealing that he wasn't Superman never diminished my admiration for him. It actually taught me what a father is.

To my kids, I'll say this: I will never be perfect, but I will always do my best to show you what a good father looks like and teach you what I know. I promise to show you my love always and forever.

To my dad, I'll say this: You were always enough. You still are.

Think of an experience where either of your parents showed you that they are human. How will you show your children the same? Would you do things differently?

56

Guilt-Free Parenting

I'm exhausted by my children who constantly need my full attention. My full attention watching a monster truck do the same flip twenty times over a cardboard box. My full attention watching the fifteenth cartwheel or the third puppet show in the last five minutes. I'm exhausted by these children who need me to get them another snack because they didn't like the first one. Who need me to help them burn off energy so they'll finally fall asleep. Who need me to sit beside them through a bedtime routine they're fighting because of nightmares.

When I finally take a break, I feel guilty, like I'm selfish for not having infinite reserves of patience and energy. But the guilt dissipates as I realize I'm *allowed* to feel exhausted by being needed so completely. I'm allowed to want a breather without it diminishing my love for my kids. And what a privilege it is to be needed in this way. They are my everything. And, sometimes, they just need to go to sleep.

I played golf when I was a teenager and one summer, I spent countless hours practicing for a tournament. On tournament day, I was burned out. My mental mistakes stacked up, and frustration consumed me. My coach pulled me aside afterward and said, "Take some time off. Practice, but don't overdo it."

I took his advice, and a week later, I won my first tournament of the season. The difference wasn't skill; it was rest and self-awareness. Golf is hard, just like parenting. Even the professionals make rookie mistakes. But bad games don't make bad golfers, and bad days don't make bad parents.

Parenting is a marathon, not a sprint, and your love for your children isn't measured by how perfect you are on the hardest days. It's measured by showing up, resting when you need to, and coming back ready to try again.

Validate yourself today. Give yourself some grace and acknowledge that parenting is hard, then take a break—guilt-free—if you need one.

57

Leave the Axe Out to Rust

"The axe forgets, but the tree remembers." This African proverb is a powerful reminder of the lasting impact of our words and actions, particularly on those we love most. Have you ever brought up something hurtful someone said to you, only for them to have no memory of it? Often, it's our family—especially our parents—whose words can cut the deepest. It's usually something negative, a sharp phrase or a dismissive comment, that sticks with you for years.

When you confront someone about these moments, you might hope for an apology, or at least acknowledgment. If they refuse to recognize the injury, it can feel like trying to convince someone that it's raining, only for them to insist there are no clouds. It's frustrating, invalidating, and sometimes heartbreaking.

More often than not, our parents simply don't remember the hurtful thing they said. When cortisol, the stress hormone, runs high, short-term memory often shuts down. This is why people struggle to recall details of traumatic events. But another part of me wonders if some memories are buried intentionally, blocked out to avoid guilt or discomfort.

Regardless of intent, the truth remains: What might be a fleeting bad moment for a parent can be a lifetime memory for a child. When a parent screams, "What is wrong with you?" in a moment of frustration, it may feel insignificant by the next day. For the child, though, those words linger. They become etched into the tree rings of their being, shaping how they see themselves and their worth.

The Giving Tree by Shel Silverstein offers another lens, showing a tree who gives of herself selflessly to a boy, over and over, until nothing remains but a stump. While the story is often interpreted as one of unconditional love, it also reminds us of the importance of balance. If we give without nurturing ourselves—or if we take without showing gratitude—we risk leaving those we love with nothing.

Instead of being the axe that cuts into your child's spirit, strive to be the water that helps them grow. Nourish them with apologies when you make mistakes. Choose words that build rather than tear down. And when you feel overwhelmed, leave the axe outside to rust. Be the roots that ground them, not the storm that scars them.

Think intentionally about what words and phrases you don't ever want to say to your children.

58

I Hope You Have a Child Like You One Day

Our babies come into the world and we hear: "They're the spitting image of you," or "I see both of you in them," or even from our parents: "It's like having you all over again." We may not see ourselves physically in our kids, but we often recognize their personalities, interests, or maybe their fierce attitudes that strikingly resemble ours. Oops.

Raise your hand if you've heard the phrase *I hope you have a child like you one day,* or *Just wait until you're a parent*. It implies that we were difficult children and that our parents hope we'll see what it was like.

But let's unpack these phrases. Are they suggesting that an obedient child is an easy one? Is compliance the standard for good parenting? Is our goal to mold our kids into submissive, agreeable little humans? I'll answer this for you: No. Compliance doesn't equal good parenting, nor does it define the kind of human your child will become. Kids are often noncompliant simply because they *are* kids. Stubbornness, boundary-pushing, attitudes, and an abundance of energy are all part of the package.

I remember being a noncompliant child—always pushing boundaries. I didn't know why, but I knew it didn't make adults happy. Now, as an adult, I realize that obedience is often about fitting into what the outside world wants you to be. And no, this doesn't mean I'm encouraging disrespect or bad behavior. Let's not get carried away.

I have children who are like me and like my wife. That dreaded phrase *Wow, you're just like your mother,* used negatively to describe my daughter's attitude is a direct invitation for my wife to respond, "Are you serious right now?" Instead, I'd rather say to my daughter, "Your attitude is as fierce as your mother's, and when you grow up, you'll be just as confident, brave, and unapologetically yourself."

My son, on the other hand, is wild and fearless. His stunts often bring us closer to our insurance deductible, and in that we are identical. I don't know if these traits are genetic or just because he's a kid, but they remind me of the magic of childhood.

My wife and I grew up to have children just like us. That hope came true. And every year, when my kids blow out their birthday candles, I make a wish too—for them to keep being exactly what they are: kids growing up in this world.

Do you see traits in your children that you see in yourself or your partner? Where does compliance rate on your personal parenting scale? Why?

59

Living Room Kids

The internet-famous phrase *living room kids* refers to children who spend a lot of time with their families in the living room. Just tonight, my family and I were snugly tucked together in the living room. The coziness level was top-notch thanks to a cold front that brought the temperature outside down to 0 degrees Fahrenheit. My kids are 100 percent living room kids.

Growing up, I was a living room kid too. I always wanted to be in the mix with my older siblings. It gave me a sense of comfort, being in the living room with my family. Family movie nights were the best. I'll never forget watching *Top Gun* for the first time in the living room. My dad had just gotten new speakers for the TV and wanted to test them out. Such '90s nostalgia.

I'd argue that the living room is just as important as the

dinner table. When families start frequently retreating to different parts of the house there can be a gradual decline in closeness. Even after my parents split, when it was just my dad, my brother, and me, I found so much comfort when my brother stayed in for the night to hang out with me in the living room.

Of course, as our kids get older—and anyone with teenagers can tell you—there's a natural gravitational pull toward their bedrooms, and that's to be expected. Ironically, parents of young kids sometimes wish for that pull just so they can have a moment of alone time. But let's soak in this time with our kids wanting to be living room kids with us as long as possible.

It's easy to feel alone in a room full of people these days. The living room is a space where games are played, tears are shed, comfort is given, parties are hosted, and the core values of your family are created.

Let's raise some living room kids.

Hang out together in the living room—perhaps make it a family game night!

60

Everyone Makes Mistakes

Yesterday, I accidentally threw away one of my daughter's stuffies. Overwhelmed by my to-do list and anxious about an upcoming trip away from my family, I did what I usually do when I'm feeling out of control: I cleaned. During this purge, I threw away a box I thought was trash, but I found out later, after the trash had already been hauled away, that it had my daughter's stuffie inside.

Now, I know that material things are replaceable. I always tell my kids that. But I was so upset with myself because this mistake happened due to the absent-mindedness and chaos within my brain that I was unable to control or regulate. I knew the stuffie had been in that box, but in that moment, I forgot.

At bedtime, when I told my daughter what had happened, she cried for a bit. After the tears subsided, I lay with her in bed. The knot of guilt still lurked in my stomach even though I told her I was going to order another stuffie. My daughter said, "Dad, I know you were stressed. Everyone makes mistakes. It's okay you accidentally threw away the stuffie."

The knot in my stomach got a little looser, but suddenly there was one in my throat. After I soaked in my eight-year-old's empathetic nature, I responded with "The best part is things are replaceable, mistakes do happen—even as grown-ups—but the love we have for each other will never change."

Later, as I thought about her words, I was reminded of an old parable about a cracked pot. Each day, the pot carried water, but some of it leaked out through a crack. The pot felt like a failure until one day, the water carrier pointed out the flowers that had grown along the path. The water leaking from the pot had nourished those flowers, making the journey more beautiful.

I realized that in my mistakes and imperfections, there's a lesson for both me and my children. Like the cracked pot, what feels like failure can often lead to unexpected beauty. My daughter's forgiveness and empathy were those flowers, a reminder that love isn't about perfection. Everyone makes mistakes.

How can you teach your children that everyone makes mistakes?

61

The Beautiful Unknown

Parenting doesn't come with a manual, and even if it did, life would still find ways to throw surprises your way. There are times when I feel like I've figured it all out, moments when everything clicks. Then, almost on cue, my kids hit me with something entirely new, something I'm not prepared for. They remind me that I don't have all the answers. But isn't that the point? It's the journey, the exploration, the constant pursuit of trying to figure it out, that gives parenting so much meaning. That's also what makes life beautiful. You don't need to figure it all out, you just need to be willing to take the ride.

This philosophy is powerfully encapsulated in the Oscar-winning film *Life Is Beautiful*. The movie tells the story of Guido, a loving Jewish father, who uses his imagination and wit to protect his young son, Giosué, from the horrors of a Nazi concentration camp during World War II. It's a powerful reminder that even in life's darkest moments, love and resilience can create light.

One of the most poignant scenes in the film takes place when Guido convinces his son that their time in the camp is part of an elaborate game. Despite the unimaginable suffering they endure, Guido uses humor and play to shield Giosué from the truth, making him believe they're competing for points to win a tank. Guido whispers to his son, assuring him that everything is fine, even as the weight of their reality is crushing him.

Parenting isn't about fixing everything or knowing all the answers. It's about being present, giving your children hope, love, and security, even when you feel like the world is falling apart. We can learn from the message in *Life Is Beautiful* and Guido's example by showing up, supporting our kids, and moving forward. That's what makes parenting—and life itself—so profoundly beautiful.

Add* Life Is Beautiful *to your movie watch list if you haven't seen it. After you watch it, reflect on ways you can uniquely provide an atmosphere of security and love in your home.

62

Your Own Story

Growing up, I wanted to be either a movie director or a writer. I was obsessed with *Terminator 2*—the first R-rated movie I ever saw (at seven years old!). That movie made me fall in love with cinema. I'd act out movie scenes in my bedroom for hours. I read stories about famous filmmakers. I wrote my first short film at thirteen, a *Reservoir Dogs*–type screenplay. I'd stay up late at night writing stories, poetry, or journaling. I quit golf—despite being the best on the varsity team—to pursue what lit me up inside. I made my first short film at twenty-one, raising $7,000 to fund it. At twenty-two, I got a temp job at Sony Pictures, working for the show *Jeopardy!*.

Then in 2008, after the economy collapsed, I stopped pursuing my dreams. I chased stability instead—something that lit me up only halfway but felt more secure. Yet here

I am now, writing this book at nearly forty years old, with a job in social media content creation. I've come to realize that the definition of a "real job" is highly subjective. Our dreams don't die because we get older—they die because we listen to the lies of the world. Lies from people who aren't living your life, who say something isn't realistic, practical, or worth your time. This leads to self-doubt and fear of failure, and so we stop before we even begin.

What unrealistic dream did you have when you were younger? How does your life today line up with that? If you wish you could get back to that dream, or another, be encouraged that there is no direct, secure path in life. You are the driver, the dreamer, and the director of your own story.

There was once a kid inside you who didn't have all this noise that blurred your vision of the dreams you had. Most kids live a lifetime before realizing they had it right all along. This is your chance to break free and get back to those passions that light you up inside.

What was your "unrealistic" dream?
Are you pursuing it or was it left behind?

63

Seasons

Sometimes it seems like just yesterday that my wife and I felt like we were drowning in early parenthood. The days of trying to be productive at work with almost no sleep, the suffocation of financial worries, the irrational worst-case scenarios that constantly played in our heads, and the changing dynamic between my wife and me.

Being a parent means learning to navigate constantly changing seasons, some filled with ease and others with challenge. Children bring immeasurable joy—their innocence, their laughter, their very presence adding so much value to your life. But with that joy comes chaos, disrupted schedules, mess, and the persistent guilt that you're not doing enough. When we go through these tough seasons, it shapes us into the parents we are today. We can survive and learn from those seasons, and when we do, we shouldn't forget them. Both my kids were, ironically, born during the darkness of winter. Despite that season, both literally and figuratively, summer came, and the sun shone again.

After the dormancy of winter comes the blossoms of spring. Maybe you need the reminder today that, sometimes, what feels like the end is actually the beginning of growth. The sun will shine again.

What season are you in right now? If you're in a hard season, double down on taking care of yourself. Eat healthy, exercise, drink water, do everything that's in your control and remember: It's just a season.

64

Nothing Like a Good Mosh Pit

I've been in a few mosh pits in my time. When I was younger, I was very small for my age, and I would get destroyed in mosh pits. But I kept going back, fueled by the energy, the music, and the camaraderie that comes with the chaos. As a grown man, I've been to a handful of concerts where I partook in the infamous pit. It's still wild, sweaty, and occasionally bruising—but now, I have a new favorite pit. It's not at concerts anymore, it's at home with my kids.

Almost daily, my son and I—and sometimes my daughter joins in—create our own pit. We lay out the soft mat, bring out the bean bag, crank up some '90s heavy metal, and we mosh! It's calculated rough play at its finest. There are rules: We respect boundaries, limits, and safety. Most of all—this goes for adult mosh pits too—we respect each other. That mutual respect is key, and it's one of the things I've always appreciated about a good mosh pit.

This isn't just about a millennial metalhead dad's nostalgia. It's a bonding experience, a teaching moment, good for my mental health and my soul. My kids are learning to feel the music, to let their energy out in a healthy way, and to understand the balance between fun and safety. Sharing my love for music while engaging in playful interaction with my children warms my metalhead heart in ways I didn't know were possible.

One day, when my kids are older and my knees are questionable, I hope we can share one of life's great experiences together at a concert: THE PIT. Until then, I'll savor every chaotic, sweaty, joy-filled moment in the little pit we've created at home.

Take some time today to rough play, run around, or just let loose with your kids. It doesn't have to be perfect or planned—just intentional.

65

Sticks and Stones

Maybe you also grew up with the playground taunt "Sticks and stones may break my bones, but words will never hurt me." We all know words *do* have power. And the ones that sting the most come from the people who are supposed to be your biggest supporters: your parents.

A parent's words can build their child up or dim their flame. And if you keep dimming their flame, eventually, it will burn out. I'm not talking about yelling at your kid when you're upset or when they aren't listening. I'm talking about saying things like "Why can't you be more like [someone else]?" or "Children should be seen and not heard." These words cut deep because they are the ones that make our kids feel unworthy of our love. They leave scars—scars so permanent that when we have children of our own, we ask ourselves how any parent could say such things to their child.

Our words as parents matter so much. We all have those stressful moments when we lash out at our children, but the difference comes when we apologize. Even if our children remember the words that hurt them, they'll also remember our efforts to repair it, to make it better, to sincerely apologize. That's what prevents scarring. That's what stops your bad day from turning into your child's lifelong memory of how those words hurt worse than any sticks or stones.

Next time stress or overwhelm gets the best of you, make a point to sit down with your child afterward and explain it to them. Let them know it was just a bad moment, that it's because of the stressor, not them, and apologize if needed.

66

A Blank Piece of Paper

Picture your life as a blank piece of paper. As soon as you're born, the paper starts to fill with words and drawings depicting the events of your life, some beautiful and some ugly or painful. As adults, we sometimes look back at the drawings of our childhood and want to erase parts, cover them up, or throw the entire piece of paper away.

The beauty of parenthood is that we don't have to give our children the same piece of paper. They start with their own blank sheet, and we give them the freedom to draw their own lines, guiding them to avoid making the same mistakes we did. Because while one of the best parts of parenthood is watching your children become a version of you through their talents, interests, and qualities, an even better part is watching them become a *better* version of you. Your paper may show a lack of confidence when you entered a room as a child, but those memories are healed as you watch your child walk in with their head held high, ready to take on any challenge. Your paper may depict adults telling you to be practical about your dreams, that they were as unrealistic as the Saturday morning cartoons you watched every weekend while eating a bowl of Fruity Pebbles, but those memories are replaced as your heart lights up like E.T.'s, hearing your child's pursuits for their future.

All the memories that are recorded on your paper, memories of not being good or pretty enough or measuring up to others' expectations, fade away when you see the story your child is writing on theirs. The little human you created is a healed version of you. You suddenly feel butterflies in your stomach that you haven't felt in decades as your child becomes a version of someone you only dreamed of becoming.

What does the healed version of yourself look like? If you could fill in the blank paper with the childhood you wanted for yourself and want for your children, what would that look like?

67

Dance Parties

One night my daughter was telling me about being left out at school that day and how it had made her feel terrible. I started to give her some advice, but then I had an idea. I put on some Taylor Swift and started dancing. If I had given her all the American Girl dolls in the world, I don't think it would have made her smile as big as she did the moment she saw her dad break out into less-than-mediocre dance moves. Whatever those girls at school said or however they made her feel didn't matter anymore—it was dance party or bust now. The pop melodies and sporadic dance moves cured all the bad feelings from the day.

I know my kids aren't always going to want to dance with me, but while they do, I'm leaning into the opportunities to have as many dance parties as possible. Legendary actor and dancer Gene Kelly once said, "You dance love, and you dance joy, and you dance dreams.." I couldn't agree more.

The other night, my wife and I were cleaning up after dinner when my daughter commanded Alexa to play a song. We stopped what we were doing and we danced as a family. My son, who dances in mosh pit style, made circles around the kitchen while flailing his arms, my daughter did her signature "ballet bliss" moves, my wife went back to the club in '06, and I did the "lean back." All listening to different rhythms in our different dancing worlds, yet all simultaneously connected, we danced. Free at last.

Have a dance party with your family today!

68

Do You Feel Like a Good Dad?

Do I feel like a good dad? It depends on the day. Some days I feel like I have this whole fatherhood thing down—like I figured out the formula for a hard math equation and now it's just plug and play. Then BAM! Something happens, and suddenly I'm a short-tempered, irritable, non-present, selfish dad who's lost his flow. I couldn't wait to put my kids to bed, and then, looking into their sweet, innocent faces, guilt floods my veins like a dam breaking. Damn. They're just kids and I'm the adult. Why can't I be on top of my game every day?

The thing I've learned is that there's nothing linear about parenting. Just because I feel like things are going well one day doesn't mean it'll be the same the day after. Nor is there some "perfect" day of parenting waiting to be found. The day I wake up and hit a home run in the form of morning kisses, words of encouragement, hugs out the door, and a bedtime routine smoother than Jimi Hendrix's 1969 rendition of the national anthem is a fantasy. The goal isn't to always feel like a good dad, it's to accept that we won't always.

So do I feel like a good dad? Overall, yes, I do. I feel like a good dad because deep down in my soul, I want to be. That intention flows through me like electricity, and even though I don't put up 81 points every game, I never quit. I show up to practice despite Allen Iverson saying practice doesn't matter. It does, and even though I have bad games, I learn. Then, I rinse and repeat.

There will be days when we feel good about our performance, and there will be days when we don't. Being a dad is not linear. Reflect and accept.

69

A Man of Character

My grandfather used to give me this advice: "Do what's right, even when it's not the 'right' thing to do." My dad took this and added, "Do what's right even when no one's looking." These simple yet effective words of wisdom are what I want to pass down to my children, and hopefully they pass on to theirs.

My grandfather was a WWII Navy veteran, a Los Angeles sheriff, a husband of seventy-five years (just six days before he passed at the age of ninety-nine), and a father to three children. I looked up to him as a man of character and integrity, someone I wanted to be like.

As a sheriff in Los Angeles during the 1950s, he faced situations where doing the right thing went against societal norms or expectations—but he still chose to do the right thing. As a husband, he lit up every time he talked about my grandma. The way he called her "the most beautiful woman I've ever seen," and the way he treated the love of his life is nothing short of the greatest love story of all time (sorry, *The Notebook*).

My grandpa was special, with a smile and laugh that could light up the darkest of rooms. The last time I talked to him, two days before he went to sleep forever, I told him I was writing a book. In true Gramps fashion, he smiled and said, "Good for you, kid! Let me know when it's out so I can buy it!" Well, Gramps, you may not have been able to read it, but the world will, and I hope to continue your legacy in a way that touches the lives of others.

Always do the right thing.

Do you have a person who impacted your life? How will you continue their legacy? Reflect on this today.

70

I'm Here

In the movie *The Passion of the Christ,* Jesus carries the cross on his back, broken, beaten, and bloody. He struggles to walk another step and falls to the ground in exhaustion. His mother, Mary, watches in unimaginable pain as her son attempts to walk in agony on the way to his death. She flashes back to Jesus as a young boy, falling. She runs over to comfort him and looks into his young face, saying, "I'm here." The scene shifts back to the present, and the mother in her can't help but run to her now thirty-three-year-old son, seeking to comfort him again. She grabs his bloody face, looks into his broken, confused eyes, and says, "I'm here."

Whatever your religious beliefs, there's no denying the power of this scene. It resonates deeply with the universal desire to protect our children from pain, no matter how old they get. As my children grow up, I know I'll always remember that first fall, the first broken bone, the first time another child said something mean to them, the first time I saw that look of defeat in their eyes—it hurts to watch them experience the darker sides of the world. But beyond offering comfort, we also teach them the skills they need to overcome adversity.

When they're young, it's easy to soothe them, protect them, and ensure they know we've got their backs. As they grow, we want to do the same, but it's different. We want them to step out of their comfort zones. We want them to have the resilience and confidence to face life's problems on their own. We spend years gradually teaching them these lessons, preparing them to go out into the world. But there's still going to be this innate desire to protect our children.

We teach them those skills and then watch as they put them to use, sometimes falling along the way. At first, we want to rush over and help them up, but we hold back. Instead, we watch as they get to their knees, then their feet, and then start to walk again. We're not abandoning them as they develop their armor for the world. We've already taught them how to use the sword, and now, from a distance, we watch as they gain the strength to swing it. No matter what struggles they encounter in life, I want my kids to always know when I look them in the eyes that I'm here.

How will we assure our children that we are here for them? How can we have their backs while giving them agency?

71

I Just Don't Give a Care

What will they think of me? Everyone has struggled with what other people think of them at some point. The rapper Eminem has a song where he is telling the world he doesn't care what people think about him. I had a lot of teenage angst, so it was no surprise I wanted so badly to adopt that attitude. The problem was, I did give a lot of cares, and it prevented me from stepping out and doing what I really wanted; I was afraid of how I'd be perceived.

Flash forward to today, as I play that Eminem record for my children. I'm joking! But I still don't want my children to be defined by the opinions of others. I also don't want them to be defined by *my* opinion. When they accomplish something, of course I tell them I'm proud of them. I try to tell them that every single day. I also ask how the accomplishment makes them feel because I want them to be proud of *themselves*. I want them to develop that self-love that will burn so hot, no one will be able to put it out.

Raising children who live their lives without obsessing over external validation and instead focus on internal validation is powerful. That's a human being who isn't scared to go after their dreams, who pushes against boundaries and unpopular narratives for the greater good, who is unapologetically themselves. Those people change this world for the better.

What will they think of me? As a father, I still don't care.

If you find yourself caring about what others think, how can you focus on internal validation?

72

Breaking the Cycle

As I mentioned earlier, I've struggled with substance abuse since I was thirteen years old. Even though I got sober on January 2, 2023, I still fear that I have a genetically addictive personality that will be passed on to my children. My grandfather on my mom's side died of liver cirrhosis from alcohol at the age of sixty-three. It makes me wonder: Are my kids going to have this invisible, magnetic pull toward the dark world of inebriated bliss? How can I break the cycle of this genetic blemish?

It starts by viewing my experience with substance abuse as a strength, not a weakness. It has given me a heightened awareness and understanding that I use to inform my conversations and interactions with my kids. I might even have some sort of unofficial PhD in "Are they high?" because I'll always be able to tell! Sure, my children won't get away with using drugs, but that's not the most important thing. It's the fact that I know *why* someone would want to embark on a brain-cell-killing rampage. I know how to communicate with that desire. I know how to prevent it, and I know how to show them why their life is better without it.

I believe every personality may be prone to certain behaviors, but if I can lead by example, be honest about my mistakes from the past, have open communication with my children, and be their safe space of knowledge as to why things are the way they are, maybe the genetic blemishes could disappear faster than a zit in a Clearasil commercial.

How are you breaking the cycle?

73

Stop the Thoughts

Ah, childhood, when your biggest worries were about who you were going to play with, which candy you wanted, how late you could stay up, and, for a certain generation, the joy of Bagel Bites, Blockbuster, and *GoldenEye 007* on Nintendo 64. Those were the simple days—easily amused, and the excitement, oh, the excitement. The kind that made your heart race, filled your stomach with indescribable feelings, and made you talk at double speed.

Then we become adults, with responsibilities and jobs and children who depend on us. It's only natural that worry would come with it as well. I won't list all the things we worry about because that, in itself, makes me worry. We know exactly what keeps us up at night and why we have monthly subscriptions of melatonin. If there were a pill that brought back that childlike happiness—that stomach feeling—I'd take it. As long as the side effects weren't like one of those commercials where they mention the benefits in ten seconds but take thirty seconds to talk about death, nosebleeds, and potential loss of limbs.

If only it were easy to stop intrusive thoughts that my child is going to fall down the stairs and break their neck, or someone in a mysterious white van will offer them candy, or a car will speed down the street . . . Crap, I wasn't going to list these worries.

At night, I like to go for a run. I run from these thoughts until the only thing I can focus on is the burning in my lungs and the tightness in my calves. I plunge myself into 40-degree water and look up at the stars, sometimes spotting a meteor or a satellite drifting through the night sky. I've tried countless breathwork videos on YouTube—very earthy and very effective. I've watched *Gilmore Girls* over and over. There's something about that show that lowers my heart rate and gives me a good feeling. Kind of like the feeling of childhood—warm and fuzzy. When those things don't work and I start going down a dark hole, I remind myself that most of the things I've worried about have never happened.

From one worried parent to another, my advice to you is this: Realize that intrusive thoughts are normal. We're all experiencing them. Acknowledge they exist and find ways to combat them. Whatever your go-to is for taming the thoughts, do it as often as possible.

Think about everything you've worried about that never happened. Do you easily go down that path of worry? Remind yourself of this fact.

74

Health Is Wealth

I've been fortunate that I haven't had many physical ailments. I've had minor injuries due to working out, but other than that, I was healthy until April 2024. My family and I went out to dinner when suddenly I felt like I was getting sick. Maybe it was allergies, maybe something I ate. That night I woke up sweating—not the kind where the collar of your shirt is a little damp, my entire shirt, pillow, and sheets were soaked through to the mattress. I was shaking from what I assumed was a fever and the fact that I was drenched.

The next morning, I felt awful—no energy, a fever of 102, and a bizarre headache that felt like someone was pulling my hair. I figured I'd caught some sort of virus, probably COVID or something similar. Three COVID tests, a flu test, and a strep test all came back negative. I thought I'd just wait it out.

Five nights of sweating, shaking, and fever persisted. Then came the alarming part: I broke out in a blistery rash on my forearms and ankles. Time to go to the doctor. A Google search, as always, showed everything from bacterial infections to cancer to impending death—or maybe just a virus. The doctor treated me for a tick-borne illness called Rocky Mountain spotted fever—one of the most common causes of death from a tick bite. Going eight days untreated has led people to their graves. I was on day six.

That night, I started an antibiotic. I also had a panic attack that woke me up at 10 P.M. My heart rate was 145–165 bpm, my blood pressure was through the roof, and a new rash had appeared on my neck. Something wasn't right. After a sleepless night, I headed to the emergency room. They told me it was anxiety due to my fever, and my blood work came back fine along with a negative test for Rocky Mountain spotted fever.

The next two months were the worst health scare of my life. My rash would dissipate, leaving scars, my fever would stop, my night sweats would subside but not go away entirely, and I would have countless doctor visits only to get no answers. Autoimmune? No. Tick-borne? Negative for four different tests. Cancer? No. Bacterial infection? Possibly, but no answers as to what kind or what caused it. Then, the worst part happened.

A little over a week after the first symptoms began, I woke up with arthritic pain in my joints. I could barely get out of bed. What was happening? This continued for seven weeks, filled with enough ibuprofen to be mistaken for breath mints, inflammation so bad that my eyes hurt, losing fifteen-plus pounds, a resting heart rate of 90–100 bpm (usually 65), and countless nos to my children because Daddy was incapable. Ouch.

After I finally went on two rounds of steroids, my inflammation went away. I was better. What was it? No clue. The experience showed me how life can come at you like that. One day you can be healthy, and the next day you can't even pick up your kids. In the midst of this unknown illness, I made a promise to myself: to never take my health for granted. Work on my health daily, but never—and I mean never—take my ability to live a healthy life for granted. Also, these kids are getting picked up and carried until I break.

If you've been blessed with good health, take a moment to be grateful. If there are ways you could improve your health, it's time to start challenging yourself to take better care of yourself.

75

Come as You Are

My first cassette was Nirvana's *Nevermind.* I was eight years old, and I got it a year before Kurt Cobain tragically took his own life at the age of twenty-seven. Starting in the early '70s, people took notice of how many famous musicians and actors had passed away at the same age, and it became a group known as the 27 Club. There was a time in my life when this idea was disturbingly attractive to me—going out like a rock star. The lack of self-worth and complete emptiness I felt in my early twenties could only be explained by songs like "Something in the Way"—a somber, haunting melody, and one of Kurt Cobain's most emotionally raw vocal performances. Eventually, I dug myself out of that hole, and maybe not so coincidentally, I met my wife two months after my twenty-seventh birthday.

When my daughter was about three years old, she

spotted the altered Nirvana smiley on the cover of *Rock-abye Baby!: Lullaby Renditions of Nirvana*. We listened to it almost every night before bed. Then we started drawing the smiley on notes. We even bought matching shirts and wore them whenever we went on a "date." The symbol, whose meaning Kurt never fully explained, became a secret signature between us—a kind of *I love you*. Now eight years old herself, her love for Nirvana still holds strong.

A few years back, I got a tattoo of the Nirvana smiley on my arm, along with roses and my daughter's name. It's something so important to me that I wanted it stamped into my flesh forever. It's a reminder to myself that I'm still here, living my dream, with an amazing family. I have made the journey from despair and lacking self-worth to accepting myself, flaws and all. I've made it well beyond the 27 Club, and no matter how hopeless life can feel, I know that it gets better.

Now my son is involved in the tradition, and all three of us wear our Nirvana shirts when we go out together. Both of my kids immediately took a liking to the song "Come As You Are." Most Nirvana lyrics won't resonate with children, for good reason, but this song is about the struggle for self-acceptance. It's something I hope my children won't have to wrestle with, as I raise them to learn from my mistakes and to truly value the incredible people they are becoming. The past is over and done—come as you are, now.

Do you accept yourself for who you are?
Do you like who you are? Why or why not?

76

The Clueless Dad Stereotype

What's my child's teacher's name? Where do they go to the dentist? Who bought these Christmas gifts? Who's going to buy their Halloween costume? I thought their mom signed the permission form for the field trip? Ah, the clueless dad stereotype. We see it all the time in our favorite dads on TV shows and in movies. Think Homer Simpson, Al Bundy, Clark Griswold, or Phil Dunphy, exaggerated portrayals of clueless, bumbling fathers.

There is some truth in why dads are viewed this way. Even today, when dads are way more involved in family life than in previous generations, the stereotype lingers—that dads aren't fully "aware." That they don't concern themselves with the details of running a household or the day-to-day logistics of our kids' lives.

I laugh along at all those TV dads staring outside at a

storm or admiring a freshly mowed lawn, and, of course, staining the hell out of some white New Balances. But to find it funny that a dad is constantly annoyed by his children, has no clue about the inner workings of the household, and sees the best part of his day as sitting on the couch, alone, beer in hand, doesn't line up with how most of us dads view our role, and therefore shouldn't be the standard for fatherhood.

Dad jokes make up about 1 percent of what it means to be a dad. The other 99 percent is how hard we work to provide for, protect, guide, and be involved in every aspect of our children's lives. This is what the stereotype misses.

Of course, there are plenty of pop culture portrayals that get it right. Jack Pearson, played by Milo Ventimiglia in *This Is Us,* may be one of the most celebrated portrayals of a great dad. The show does a great job of showing not just the highs, but also the struggles of fatherhood. Jack is deeply flawed, yet he's also deeply present.

In the movie *The Pursuit of Happyness,* Chris Gardner, played by Will Smith, is a struggling single dad who endures homelessness while taking care of his son. No matter the circumstances, his dedication as a father comes first.

And long before Jack or Chris, there was Atticus Finch. *To Kill a Mockingbird* gave us a rare, countercultural image of a Depression-era father who was emotionally intelligent, morally grounded, and deeply invested in raising his children with empathy and truth. I choose to look to these examples as ones I want to emulate.

I love comedy. And what makes comedy great is often the truth hidden inside the joke. But I don't relate to the clueless dad stereotype, because I'm far from it. If you're reading this, I'm willing to bet you are too.

What is your favorite fictional portrayal of a dad? What characters do you look up to as the father you'd like to be?

77

Holding On to Who We Are

Our identities are made up of more than just being a parent. We've all had passions, hobbies, and interests that have brought fulfillment to our lives, especially when we were children. Some of these never go away. My love for music, writing, filmmaking, movies, fitness, nature, and books have been constants throughout my life. And all these identities, so to speak, still live inside me. But do I bury them because my new identity is *Dad*? Do I stop partaking in these pursuits because they take away from my role as a parent? Aren't these identities part of what makes me the dad I am today? I prioritize my role and responsibilities as a dad and husband over other interests and hobbies while I'm in this stage of life. But is it okay for my whole identity to be wrapped up in parenting?

Just because I don't have the time to watch twelve

movies in a weekend anymore or go to a concert whenever I want, doesn't mean these interests need to disappear from my life. These things are what make us who we are.

What's more, our interests can influence our children's interests and identities—like my daughter's love of Nirvana, or my son's interest in sports. Of course, letting them develop their own interests is essential, but as your kids watch you light up when you're doing something you love, it'll excite them to want to know more. Have you noticed how the children of an actor or professional athlete often follow in their footsteps? They believe it's possible because their parent did it. When someone breaks a world record or accomplishes something that was once thought impossible, others often follow because they start to believe in themselves more.

Don't let your past identities go, and don't let the passionate child inside you die. Expose those passions and, just maybe, your children will carry them on.

What was your identity before kids? What is it now? How can you participate in some of your interests and your kids' interests right now?

78

Legacy of Kindness

Kindness is often dismissed as weakness in a world that values toughness, speed, and success over connection. Yet I believe that the enduring power of kindness far outweighs the fleeting nature of success. The world will always be harsh, but we have the choice to soften it. What legacy do we want to leave behind?

One day after school, my daughter told me how she'd seen a girl crying. She didn't know this girl or why she was upset, but it made my daughter feel sad. "That happens to me a lot," she said. "I feel what others feel, even if it has nothing to do with me." I explained to her that what she feels is called empathy. "It's a gift," I told her. "It allows you to treat people the way you'd want to be treated, even if they're strangers."

Her words made me think: Do children have more

empathy than adults? Are they born with an abundance of compassion that fades over time, lost to the demands of growing up? It seems we adults often trade empathy for self-preservation, becoming more focused on ourselves and less on others. But it doesn't have to be that way. Empathy, like kindness, is a muscle we can strengthen—if we choose to.

As a parent, I hope to lead by example, showing my children that empathy is a strength, not a burden, and that kindness is something to continue to develop, not lose as we grow older. These qualities aren't just for passing moments of goodness, they're the foundation of meaningful lives and relationships. By choosing compassion and understanding in our daily interactions, we can teach our children that empathy and kindness are what truly make us strong.

The world will always have its harsh edges, but we don't have to add to them. Let's be the ones who soften them. Let's inspire our children to hold on to their natural empathy and lead with kindness. Because when each of our cards is pulled and the story of our lives is told, what could be more powerful than leaving a legacy of kindness?

Do your children see the kindness you show others? Today, look for an opportunity to show kindness in front of them, such as giving money or food to someone in need or helping an elderly person at the grocery store.

79

Let Your Children Challenge Your Beliefs

I've spoken to adults who have less wisdom than people a third of their age. Years on this planet do not necessarily equate to wisdom, intelligence, or experience. Here's the beautiful part: We can learn so much from one another if we humble ourselves to the idea that just because we are older doesn't mean we know everything.

I grew up believing in some things as absolute truths, such as religious beliefs and various values, not necessarily because I genuinely believed them, but because my parents told me, "This is how it is." There was no room for disagreement, no room to explore if there might be other ways of understanding, believing, and acting.

As a parent, I want to learn from my children. I may not always understand or agree with them, but it's important to me that I'm open to what they have to say. Parents can be so focused on molding children to fit their own beliefs, ideals, and worldviews that they never let their kids explore and develop their own. This is not the same as letting your children do whatever they want, as if you're trying to be a cool friend and not the parent who has had more life experience. Absolutely not. We can guide them, express our opinions, share our absolute truths, and, most importantly, lead by example.

I want to be open to my children challenging my beliefs, open to understanding theirs, and avoid putting my kids into the box of my own worldview without letting them explore their own.

Were there any absolute truths you weren't allowed to question as a kid? How are you going to let your kids explore their own truths?

80

Raising Kids in a Digital World

I grew up without the internet, yet saw it develop before my eyes. This shaped my understanding of the world in a unique way, as it did for my whole generation. It meant that if we wanted to play with a friend, we would ride bikes, skateboards, or rollerblades miles from home to knock on the friend's door, because that was the only way to see if they were home. We got embarrassed by our parents who picked up the second landline receiver, unaware that we were on the phone with our crush. We dug holes to China, we played with roly-polies, and we traded Pogs. As teenagers, we went to garage parties with nothing but red Solo cups, a table, Ping-Pong balls, and music blaring from a CD on someone's boom box. Our formative years were mostly analog, and we weren't consumed by everything happening in the world being available at our fingertips.

Each generation of parents has had to navigate technological advances and how their kids interact with them. In the twentieth century, parents began to fear "brain rot," first as television made its way into homes, then as videogames became more prevalent, and now with so many opinions about how much screen time is too much. Concerns over the type of entertainment kids were being exposed to—from MTV and *Beavis and Butt-Head* to *South Park,* and, later, the internet opened up new fears about chat rooms and access to pornography. With the advent of smartphones and social media, and now the brand-new frontier of generative AI, the world looks very different in the twenty-first century, as we all race to keep up with what new technology means for mental health, education, relationships, careers, and more.

As parents, it's our job to teach our kids how to interact with technology. Technology can make life easier and more fun—having any song ever recorded ready to blast from a Bluetooth speaker is awesome! It's also the reality of the world our kids will be entering as they grow into adults. Yet there can be a dark side to what can be accessed, and how it can be used to harm them.

What if we leaned into the millennial nostalgia, as people who have lived in both an analog and digital world, to show our kids that balance is possible? What if we could give our kids a taste of the '90s childhood, so to speak, and guide them through this technological age?

Because one day, your child will remember what their childhood felt like. And I want mine to remember warmth.

Laughter. Connection. Boredom, even. Not just the glow of a screen.

Let's bring back the best parts of childhood.

Let's create a new normal worth remembering.

What good habit around technology use (e.g., screen time) do you want to establish and model for your kids?

81

The Weight We Carry

Does this sound familiar to you: "Dad, you are in control of the household today. Your attitude, mood, and the way you carry yourself will set the tone for the day. It's a burden you carry, one that doesn't go away, and no, you can't take a break. Dad, you can't burn out—you're DAD. Don't you dare talk about this. Keep it to yourself. They're counting on you."

That's the internal message many dads hear every day. I've heard a version of this message playing on repeat many times since becoming a father, something like: "There are children who are starving. There are families dealing with cancer. You aren't dealing with anything half as hard. Shut your dumb mouth and keep your chin up." I took pride in this "grind it out" mentality, this "tough love" from my inner critic.

To be honest, I'm done with this whole "grind it out because that's what men are made to do" mindset. That mindset is broken. I'm done with the "suffer in silence" narrative we push as a masculine society. Men are not built to carry all this weight on our shoulders forever. Sure, we can deal with some knots in our necks and traps, but when that disc starts slipping—ouch.

It's time for us to change the inner message to this: "Dad, I want you to know how important you are. Yes, there is a joyful burden you carry. You have a job to do, and it's more than important—it's vital. Your kids are counting on you, and they need you here for a long time. But, Dad, you deserve to be okay, too. You deserve to carry the weight with the right support, so it feels lighter. Some days, it's inevitable that the load will be harder to bear."

Today, Dad, I need you to do something for me. Take five minutes to just *be*. Just be in this moment and know deep in your heart—the same heart that burns for your family—that you're going to be okay. You're going to be all right.

How do you feel today, Dad? You are so important to your family dynamic and I want you to give yourself some affirmations that validate that. "You are the backbone." "You are built for this." "You are important, you are needed, and you are going to conquer this day."

82

Who Will We Be When They Figure Us Out?

One day, our children will figure us out. I would love to live in this bubble of childlikeness with them forever—the days when they run into my arms without a care in the world, shouting, "Daddy!" at the top of their lungs. The way they trust so easily, the safety net that is Dad. I would love to stay here, wrapped in their belief that I'm the strongest, wisest, most unflawed man they know. But the truth is, one day, they'll get older. One day, they'll start to see me for who I really am.

Before they see through the cracks, before the veil lifts, we're writing the story of who we are in their lives. Every moment we're present, or not, every time we choose patience over anger—or anger over patience—every hug, every promise kept or broken, is building their perception of who we truly are. We may not realize it, but we're always showing them the answers to the questions they don't know they'll one day ask: Can they count on us? Will we be there when it matters most? Will they see us as someone who stood by them, or someone who let them down?

When they're little, maybe we can get away with more. They forgive easily, they forget quickly. But when they're older, when they've grown and seen enough of the world to know better, they'll see the truth. They'll figure us out, flaws and all. And the real question is, what kind of person will they discover? Will they find someone who was there? Or someone who was absent more than they were present? Will they see someone who tried their best, even when they stumbled, or someone who let their frustrations and fears rule over love? These are the things that matter—not some idealized version of ourselves we can never truly maintain. Presence. Dependability. Effort.

Because in the end, they won't need perfection from us. They'll need to know that we were there, that we were real. They'll need to know that we loved them through our mistakes, that we showed up in the messiness of life, and that we did our best, even when it wasn't pretty.

When our children figure us out, it won't be the end of their love for us. It will be the beginning of a deeper understanding, a realization that love isn't about seeing someone as flawless—it's about loving them despite their flaws. And when that time comes, I hope my children will look at me and see someone who was present, someone who tried, someone who, above all, loved them unconditionally.

Our children will figure us out. The question is who they'll find when they do.

What's the first thing that comes to mind when you think of your parents? How does that make you feel? Write down five adjectives you hope your children will include in their list when describing you.

83

Parenting First, Marriage Always

My wife and I have made the choice to put our children before our marriage—for now. Before you burn me at the stake, let me clarify: I'm not saying I'm putting the *importance* of my marriage behind my kids, nor am I letting our marriage decline because of our kids. It's just that raising children takes more work than maintaining a marriage. Let's be honest here—parenting a little human from scratch takes more energy than the work required between two adults. It's a different kind of work.

I'll be up front with you: It's been a long time since my wife and I slept alone in our bed. A lot of times we don't even sleep in the same bed. Has this impacted our intimacy, our connection, or our time spent together? No, not really. There are other rooms in the house for intimacy.

(Maybe that's TMI, but I'm willing to bet I'm not the only one in this situation.) The point is, our kids being in our bed isn't something that bothers us. It won't be like this forever. Eventually, they'll sleep on their own. Eventually.

I take my daughter and son out for one-on-one time more often than I do my wife. When we're not with the kids individually, we're all together as a family. Do my wife and I have date nights? Yes, but not that often. Are we alone together as much as we used to be? No, but honestly, that's okay for now. I can say with all my heart that our marriage is still solid, even though our kids take up most of our time.

One day, it will be just the two of us again. We acknowledge that, and we make sure to nurture that part of our relationship, knowing that we need to protect it for the future. But for now, it's our kids before our marriage. When you have a partner who's equally invested in parenting, works with you as a team, communicates well, and is just a damn good parent, it works.

Good parenting and a strong marriage can both be true at the same time, but one is definitely harder than the other.

How do you view marriage in this stage of life?

84

Chasing Enough

In my mid-thirties, I accomplished a lot of my goals. Financial gain, a beautiful house, and the dream of becoming a writer. Then, a few years later, I started thinking about what else I needed to accomplish in order to feel content. I'd think, "When [fill in the blank] happens, I'll finally be able to relax."

Listen to me carefully: There is always more to accomplish. There is always something more to do. (We can often feel this way about our parenting too.) Success will not fill the void you think it will, whether it's due to insecurity, a childhood where you never felt good enough, or any other underlying issue you think money, success, fame, or recognition will solve. If anything, it makes it worse. Don't make me quote The Notorious B.I.G. here—"mo money . . ." you finish it for me.

I feel obligated to say the obvious here: There's nothing wrong with chasing objectives, having goals, yada yada yada. Just make sure you also celebrate the wins, accept what cannot be controlled, live in the moment, and pat yourself on the back every once in a while.

You could write a whole book about why you don't feel like you're doing enough, why you're never proud of yourself, why you are never content, or why you always look to the future. But here's the thing: None of it's true. You've made it up, and it's only real because you've convinced yourself it is. No, I'm not about to dive into the theory that we're living in a simulation—there are enough podcasts on that already. I'm talking about your mind. It does what it's told. It believes what it's told. I teach my kids about words of affirmation, yet here I am telling myself I'm a piece of garbage because I'm not doing as well as so-and-so. That's a terrible mindset, and it's time to change it. Start small and start with your mind.

Are you content? Why or why not? What mental shift might need to happen for you to find contentment?

85

A Voice to Be Heard

Most people do not listen with the intent to understand; they listen with the intent to reply.

—Stephen R. Covey

There's one thing you can put into practice that, no matter how much or how often you do it, when you do it, or who you do it with, is always a good idea: listening. Listening doesn't come naturally to me. I have to continually remind myself to do it more. When I'm in a conversation, I either want to talk so I don't forget, fix the issue immediately, or speak up to feel involved. These are all really bad habits when it comes to Listening 101.

The amount we can learn just from listening is astounding. We can learn about different subjects, cultures, people's habits, stories—and, most importantly, we can learn about our children. My marriage got exponentially better when I began to listen. My formerly nonlistening brain finally started to understand that I was helping and even solving problems just by the simple act of listening. I don't want to make it sound like I've figured it all out, because I know I still need to listen more. I've been practicing with my children. I've been practicing putting my phone down and listening to them, even when it's about something I don't care much about. It's never that I don't care about *them;* it's sometimes the subject they're talking about. But it's important to them, and if I want them to feel important, I need to listen no matter what. Often, they share pivotal things—how someone treated them, a proud moment, or a new discovery. Whatever it is, they need my full attention. They need me to listen. They need me to learn.

I can't promise my children their voices will always be heard by others, but I can promise they'll always be heard by me.

If you could give yourself a grade on listening, what would it be? Try listening to your child today, without distractions or interruptions. What did you learn?

86

Why Resenting Our Parents Won't Heal Us

There's a saying that I frequently see shared on social media: "As your child, I'll forgive you. As a parent, I never will." It resonates because it speaks to the lasting pain that a parent can bring to a child, and how we have to reckon with that pain when we have kids of our own. It's easy to get stuck in resenting our parents for what they did to us or how they shaped us in childhood. But that's missing the point.

The world we're born into isn't our choice. We don't get to pick it. We only get to respond to it.

When we're young, it's easier to forgive. A lot of that comes from not yet knowing what is acceptable. The yelling, the cursing, the hitting, the constant feeling that no matter what we do, our parents are rarely satisfied with us.

It all becomes part of our version of normal. But as we get older, we begin to see things differently. We compare our world to our friends' and neighbors' and realize that our normal isn't everyone else's.

Some of us come to realize that our parents are dishonest, unfaithful, or battling addiction. Others may never fully see it, because love often shields the truth. We might excuse their behavior or blame ourselves for it. We believe we fell short. That we were not enough. That we just couldn't meet the expectations set before us, no matter how hard we tried. Some of us watched our parents choose other families, new partners, or different priorities. Some of us gained siblings who share all, some, or none of our blood. And some of us had a parent who was never truly there. Maybe they left before our memories began. Or maybe they were physically present but emotionally unavailable, like a ghost we couldn't reach.

We all come from different stories. But once we become parents, we look back at the kind of parent we had and begin to understand parenting through a new lens.

We may never forget the childhood we were given. But holding on to the past will not help us be better parents today. We can recognize our parents' mistakes. We can choose a different path. We can even forgive them.

As your child, I forgive you.

As a parent, I understand that the brokenness I came from was born from your own brokenness.

I break the cycle. I let go of the weight. I refuse to pass it on.

As a parent, I won't ever forget—so that my children never have to remember.

No matter where you came from, staying consumed with your parents' mistakes will only distract you from the most important job you have—raising great human beings. Break the cycle. Be the parent worth coming back to. Let it go. Create the world your children deserve.

87

Leaving Too Early

I have a fear of dying too early. There, I said it. "Too early" is subjective, but in this case, it means leaving this world at a time when my children still need me.

One day, we all must die. Wow, great segue into positivity, right? Stay with me, please. This is the reality, and there's absolutely nothing we can do about it. Actually, there is: We can start living. That's the choice we have, and all these fears and worries are completely valid, but they don't change the fact that we need to start living. You think I'm going to go all motivational guru on you and tell you how you should go about your precious days? Hell no. Do you know what's the first thing I do when those thoughts of mortality seep into my cranium? I kiss my children, kiss my wife, and I tell them I love them. I hug them. I make sure they know these things.

My fear isn't necessarily of dying; it's that the people I love the most won't realize just how much they meant to me. Let this be your reminder to let everyone in your life who means so much to you right now know it, without a doubt. I want my children to know to always be themselves despite what others think, to dream the wildest dreams, to work hard and find joy in that, to find work that isn't work at all, to never grow up, to be kind to everyone, to be the light in the darkest of situations, and of course, that Dad loves them with every fiber, ligament, vein, and living cell in my body. They are truly my heart outside of myself.

We don't know when we're leaving, but don't let that thought dim your spirit—let it fill you with the love of time. It's so precious, so go spend it with the people who light you up. Tell those people how much they mean to you. Tell them everything you want to see them achieve, and tell them now, because *now* is what we most certainly have.

It's not the future we need to obsess over; the unknown is inevitable. What is most important for you to focus on right now?

88

Don't Grow Up, It's a Trap

The kids who live in my neighborhood love to play baseball in a cul-de-sac. Yes, with the plastic Wiffle ball bat and bases made out of random items like a T-shirt. It sounds straight out of the '90s, but I swear I didn't time travel—this is in 2025. Sometimes I'll join in, and as I approach home plate—marked by a hat—all the kids frantically spread out, some going as far back as if I'm Barry Bonds in 2001. (They may overestimate my skill, but I don't hate it!) I aim for the nearest spot that would count as a home run, risking the durability of the plastic bat.

I see dads everywhere playing with their kids. I'm impressed by all the dads chasing their little humans around the park, skateboarding, scootering, playing football, shooting hoops. Play is so important. It's good for our mental health, and it's good for our physical health. Sure, running, exercising, and weight lifting have clear benefits, but I'm talking about *playing* like we did when we were kids.

We also connect with our kids when we play with them. Spending time together, engaging with them, and eliminating distractions to be fully present in a moment of play goes a long way to showing them love in a language they speak. When I got sick a couple years ago, my body inflamed to the point where I couldn't leave my bed for weeks, and this is what I missed most. Not deadlifting or running but playing. Roughhousing with my son, turning my kids into flying superheroes by zooming them around the house in my arms.

It's easy to grow comfortable getting older. To stop getting down on the ground to play Legos, or to blame a sore back for not putting them up on our shoulders. I don't know about you, but I don't want age to slow me down when it comes to playing with my kids.

I want to always be the dad who jumps in on a game of cul-de-sac baseball, who runs up the slide when his kid yells, "You're it!" I want to always be the dad who plays with his kids, even after they grow older. Life is too short to stop playing.

Time to let loose, Dad. Don't get too comfortable growing old. Get out there and play.

89

Siblings That Become Strangers

To the outside world we all grow old. But not to brothers and sisters. We know each other as we always were.
—Unknown

The day my son was born, my then-three-year-old daughter walked into the hospital room with a new Build-A-Bear in hand, one she'd named Baby. She had recorded a message in her little voice that would play when you pressed the bear's paw, welcoming her brother to the world. With a little help, she held her new brother, looked down at him with pure joy, and kissed him gently on the forehead. That moment is etched in my heart forever.

Watching them grow as siblings comes with its share of challenges, but, like parenting itself, it brings the most rewarding experiences. I've seen the moments when my son's big sister defends him around other kids, the times when they share or even sacrifice something of their own to make the other happy. And then there are the quiet times, when they're simply playing together, just the two of them. Of course, there are struggles, too—moments when they won't share, flashes of jealousy, bickering, and fighting. But I know each of these moments, good and bad, is shaping the foundation of their bond. All these experiences, woven together, will ultimately define their relationship as they grow older.

I've known siblings who grow up and drift apart—not in the natural way that life sometimes pulls us in different directions, but in ways that mean they hardly speak or only reunite for family funerals. What a heartbreaking thing that would be to witness as a parent.

What causes siblings to become strangers? Is it something rooted in childhood? There isn't one answer; it's too complex to unravel. But I do know that I never want that for my kids. I want them to understand the value of family—that as they grow, build lives of their own, and even create their own families, they should never forget where they came from. I hope they carry with them the values we instill, the character we nurture, and, most importantly, the bond of unconditional sibling love.

The connection, memories, and love should remain, even if life takes them far apart. I want them to always feel, deep in their hearts, the bond they shared as children. Even if they make mistakes and set boundaries as adults, I want them to come back to the same dinner table, to look back on their childhood and say, "My best friend was my brother," or "My best friend was my sister."

No matter the twists and turns life brings, I hope that bond is one they'll always hold on to. That's the legacy I want to leave them with—to cherish, remember, and never forget the family they came from.

If you have multiple children, what can you do now to help build a bond that will keep their relationship strong?

90

Embracing the Truth

A man can fail many times, but he isn't a failure
until he begins to blame somebody else.
—John Burroughs

Accountability is one of the most important character traits. It shapes how we treat others, influences our success, and sets an example. Have you ever caught your children in a blatant lie? I remember the first time it happened with my daughter. She was so young that I knew she hadn't learned to lie from anyone else. It felt instinctive. That moment made me realize how crucial it is to stress honesty and accountability. I wasn't going to let that slipup pass without teaching her about the value of taking responsibility.

I'm convinced that if every adult took more accountability for their actions, their lives would improve. Yet, as parents, we sometimes overlook this. Not intentionally, but we don't always emphasize its importance. Too many times we bend the truth for personal gain, make excuses for poor outcomes, and avoid admitting mistakes.

We need to take charge of our own lives. We must teach our children, as early as possible, that they have control over their actions. When I catch my children in a lie, I immediately sit them down to have a conversation. We talk about why lying is never the way out and I encourage them to apologize and think through ways to prevent that from happening in the future.

Let's guide our children to find their own way, and when things go wrong, to take accountability first, make changes, and try again. There's much we can't control, but accountability—the ability to own our actions and make adjustments—is within our power. And it all starts with embracing the truth.

How are you teaching your children accountability?

91

Outcasts Are the Biggest Dreamers

You are never too old to set another goal
or dream a new dream.
—Les Brown

When I was younger, I thought I was a loser, a bad kid, an outcast. I wasted a lot of years believing I was stuck, holding on to my mistakes like baggage. I had written a story for myself that said, "I messed up my life, I'm lost, and it's too late to do anything worthwhile." That was such a lie.

I graduated high school with a 2.6 GPA. I wasn't dumb; I just hated school with all my heart. The only list I made in high school was the top three on the truancy list, with upward of seventy-five absences halfway through the school year. After high school, I watched my classmates go off to college, land high-paying jobs, and build stable lives. I went to community college, where I thrived. I earned straight A's my first year—turns out, that's what I was capable of when I actually showed up to class. It's also what happened when I started learning about subjects that truly interested me. I'd had dreams when I was younger. But as I grew older, I lost sight of those dreams.

We all had aspirations when we were young. But as we aged, people told us we were running out of time, that we should've started sooner, that our grades weren't good enough, that we weren't smart enough, or talented enough, that we needed to be realistic. As a result, we stopped dreaming and started making choices that others wanted for us, or that society expected of us. We felt the pressure to act differently, to start "acting our age." We now viewed those dreams as silly, something only for kids.

I don't know your story. I don't know if you're living out your dreams. What I do know is that the so-called losers, the outcasts, the "bad kids," and even those expected to be great can all create their own path. It's never too late to do anything, in fact, that's one of life's greatest joys. Cynics might ask if they can still play in the NFL at thirty-five instead of working a corporate job. To them, I would say, whatever mentality you choose, whatever beliefs you hold about what's possible or realistic, are yours to keep. Life is short, but it's also long.

How you chase your dreams will encourage your children to chase theirs. What are you modeling for them?

92

Boundaries

Good fences make good neighbors.
—Robert Frost

On that classic '90s sitcom *Home Improvement,* Tim Allen's character had a neighbor named Wilson who would occasionally poke half his head over the fence to share some words of wisdom. They never showed his whole face; it was always obscured by the fence, or a plant, or some random object. Wilson only showed up when Tim needed him most, and his words were often just the right amount of guidance without overstepping. His fence was both literal and figurative—a boundary that preserved respect and space in their friendship.

Wouldn't it be nice to have boundaries like that with everyone in our lives—especially family, friends, and acquaintances? Imagine not feeling guilty for being busy or pressured to constantly be available. Just advice, encouragement, and support, only when needed.

It's interesting how family dynamics can be so different. There are those who offer invaluable support, always there for their children and grandchildren. But sometimes they can overstep, visit too much, or even compete over tasks like who can make the best Halloween costume. On the other hand, there's the toxic group—the family members you wish were different. They might bring up uncomfortable topics like politics too often, drink too much at gatherings, or refuse to acknowledge past mistakes and hurts. Both groups have their complaints, but both could benefit from boundaries.

For the supportive group, boundaries aren't about keeping them out, they're about preserving the joy and respect in the relationship. It's about allowing everyone to show up for one another in ways that don't feel overwhelming. When life is good, sometimes it's human nature to find something wrong, even with those we love. Maybe it's just hard for us to be content. But boundaries can keep us grounded and allow relationships to thrive.

For the toxic group, boundaries are often a necessity, giving us room to create a safe environment for ourselves and our children. I've been told that with toxic family members, sometimes you need to set ultimatums: They can visit, but only if they stay in a hotel and keep the visit to three days. If certain behaviors happen, they'll need to leave. A boundary doesn't always have to be an ultimatum, though. Sometimes it's as simple as deciding certain topics are off-limits or setting designated times for visits. It's about creating rules that let relationships function without constant friction. And importantly, don't waste energy trying to change or reason with them; that's where we get into trouble.

It's normal to feel a twinge of guilt when setting boundaries with those who love us. But it's not about deleting them from our lives forever; it's about our space, our sanity. Sure, feelings might get hurt, but ultimately, everyone is happier and healthier with clear boundaries.

In the end, good fences don't distance us, they preserve the relationships we value. Whether it's a gentle boundary with a supportive family member or a firmer one with someone toxic, these fences allow us to connect in healthy, balanced ways—just like Wilson on the other side of the fence, there when we need him most.

How are you keeping boundaries within your family? Is it something you're doing well or does a fence need to be put up?

93

The Dark Realities

The only wisdom we can hope to acquire
Is the wisdom of humility: humility is endless.
—T. S. Eliot, "Four Quartets"

I was running errands with my children one day when we encountered a person who was sleeping on the street. My children's reaction—the way they were shocked to learn that some people didn't have a home—caught me off guard. Living in a city, you can become almost immune to the sight of people experiencing homelessness; it just fades into the background. But my children couldn't wrap their minds around the idea or how we could simply pass these people by.

I wondered if this was the moment to reveal some of the harsher realities of the world—that, for some people, life is incredibly tough and there are terrible things that happen daily, often beyond our control. Instead, I explained that these people needed help and asked my kids if they wanted to help, even just a little. Without hesitation, they said, "Yes!" So, we gave a few dollars to the person. Yet, as we later encountered other people in a similar state, my daughter didn't feel it was enough. She kept asking, "Why?"

Moments like these hit me hard. They make me reflect on the person I've become. I used to be that child, filled with empathy for the world's pain. Now I'm grown, and somewhere along the way, I became hardened to the darker realities of the world. I don't see the world as my children do anymore, and it makes me want to preserve that empathy in their hearts.

I've decided to find small ways to help my kids keep this compassion alive. Whether it's setting aside a few dollars each month to give to someone in need, volunteering as a family, or just having conversations about people's struggles, I want them to remember that life is about thinking of others, not just ourselves. Life will bring its own harsh realities, but we always have a choice: to see the world with empathy and act on it, to think of others before ourselves, and to never lose sight of the impact one small act of kindness can make.

How do you approach the harsh realities of the world with your children? The conversation will depend on your children's age, but start these conversations early.

94

A Life Made Up of Seconds

When I was twenty-seven, I moved from my birthplace in southern California to Nashville, Tennessee. I was ready for a fresh start—and, if I'm being honest, ready to meet my forever love. But after a couple months of unsuccessful and uninspiring online dates, I was losing hope.

Fall was approaching, which was one of the main things that had drawn me to Tennessee. Where I'm from doesn't really have fall—the waves get good during that time, but that's about it. Fall in Tennessee was like a scene from a movie. It was unlike anything I'd experienced before.

Not long after I moved to Nashville, my brother-in-law at the time called me. "I think I found your wife," he said. I laughed it off, assuming it was a joke because he had never tried to set me up with anyone before. "No, really. I got a haircut today and met this girl from Ohio who just moved here. I awkwardly got her Facebook info for you, if you want to message her. She had a great personality and an amazing smile."

I laughed again but agreed to send her a message. Two hours later, I texted this unknown girl. That Facebook Messenger conversation turned into a three-hour phone call, which led to a coffee date the next day. That coffee date lasted four hours, and the next night, we went out for sushi. Five months later, I was engaged to this woman. Eleven months after that Facebook message, I met her at the end of the aisle.

My wife and I often talk about how it all came down to seconds—those tiny, seemingly insignificant decisions that led to bigger ones, which ultimately led to a moment of connection. My brother-in-law decided, at the last minute, to get a haircut, and someone he ran into suggested the salon where my future wife worked. My future wife happened to work that day, when the next day was her day off. If even one of those seconds had gone differently, our lives would be completely different.

Our existence is made up of seconds. When you see life that way, you realize that everyone on Earth was meant to be here. How could they not be?

When my children tell me they're happy I met Momma because that's why they're here, I respond, "You were always supposed to be here. You're made up of seconds."

What's your story that's made up of seconds? Was it a car ride? A phone call? Take some time to really let that sink in and be grateful.

95

You're More Than Your Appearance

When I was in my mid-twenties, I desperately wanted to look like a bodybuilder. I took steroids, followed strict diets, worked out with precision, and was beyond disciplined. But when I achieved what I thought was my dream body, I felt empty. I looked in the mirror and saw a below-average physique, even a useless one. My quest had led to irresponsible steroid use, an eating disorder, and a relentless search for validation that I was "good enough." This wasn't about health; it was about trying to give myself worth—and I developed body dysmorphia in the process.

We are bombarded with images of "ideal" bodies and physical appearance. And while this is something boys and men struggle with as well (as I found out firsthand), I know how the messaging aimed at girls and women is even more pervasive. How do we protect our little girls from believing their worth lies solely in their appearance? It starts at home. Of course it does. It starts with the way the mother talks about herself, the way the father talks to the mother, and most definitely the way the father talks to his daughter. It's in how the mother talks to her daughter and how the father talks to his son.

I compliment my daughter's appearance, but I also make sure to compliment *her*—who she is. Yes, she's going to want to look good and feel good about her appearance, and that's fine, but that's not everything that makes her valuable. I want her confidence to come from the qualities that make her so special: her bravery, her kindness, her empathy, her talents—all the things that make her unique.

Think about the language you use when discussing bodies and appearance with and around your kids. Are there any shifts that would help your kids feel more confident about themselves?

96

Memento Mori

Memento mori is a Latin phrase that means *remember you must die*. I have a card that has blank bubbles you mark off, each representing a week lived. There are about four thousand bubbles that represent seventy-six years, the average life expectancy. It's inspired by modern interpretations of the memento mori philosophy. There's something unsettling about filling it out—watching those weeks fill up creates a visceral awareness of life's brevity. It forces you to ask yourself: *Am I doing this life thing correctly? How much time have I wasted?* And then the harsh truth hits: One day, you'll inevitably mark off that last bubble. One day, you're going to die.

This artistic and philosophical trope has deep roots. The Bible touches on it in Ecclesiastes 7:4: "Someone who is always thinking about happiness is a fool. A wise person thinks about death." The verse contrasts the fleeting nature of pleasure with the wisdom gained from confronting life's impermanence. It's a sobering reminder. This theme appears elsewhere, too—in seventeenth-century art and on Puritan tombstones. Skulls, hourglasses, and fading flowers were common symbols, all meant to drive home the inevitability of death. Memento mori is perhaps most famously associated with Stoicism, a philosophy that teaches us to live *because* we must die.

I like the phrase. It's edgy; it comes with heavy metal imagery of skulls and death. It's provocative—it gets people going! That said, there's a side memento mori doesn't fully explore: If we're always thinking about death and the possibility that the Grim Reaper could come knocking at any moment, how do we actually live?

Here's the thing: No one really knows when they will die. If I knew I had six months left, I would live my life entirely differently. I think everyone would. I wouldn't be working, that's for sure. I'd probably post up in the most beautiful scenery imaginable with my family. But we can't live like that all the time. Not entirely. We have responsibilities, futures to plan, and decades—hopefully—to fill. There's a balance to strike: living with the awareness of death but also with the confidence that we *might* have time.

That's not to say we should put things off as if we have forever. But we also don't need to act like every day is our last when we may have decades left. Rushing to check off a bucket list can make us forget to be content, to savor the present, and to plan wisely for the future. Life requires both mindfulness and prudence. We need to plan to live to ninety, even while remembering we're not promised tomorrow.

I still hold to the idea that we don't have the luxury of immortality, but I also recognize that life is not necessarily slipping through our fingers as quickly as we might fear. It's about balance. Don't always think about happiness, and don't always think about death. Think about *living*.

How do you receive the message of* memento mori? *Does it motivate you to live?

97

The Pursuit of Enough

I love pursuing purpose. I need purpose. For me, purpose means more than just working hard or achieving success—it's about leaving a legacy of character and showing my children what it means to live with intention. I want them to see hard work, sacrifice, and the pursuit of something meaningful. But I don't want to teach those lessons at the expense of *them*. Our intentions can be pure, but we can also drown ourselves in the pursuit and forget which way is up.

Our careers can creep ahead of our families without us even realizing it. We put our heads down and grind, falling back on the excuse "I'm doing it for the family." But where's the line between doing it for your family and doing it for yourself?

I'm not sure where the line is, but I have a feeling that

when we cross it, we'll know. The voice of denial will whisper, "No, you deserve this. Your children will understand one day." Maybe they will, maybe they won't.

I wish contentment was as sexy as the never-ending pursuit of *more*. But it's not, because in our minds, contentment feels like the end. It's where we imagine the pursuit stops, and we sit down, motionless—a slow, miserable death. But that's not what contentment really is. Contentment is continuing to pursue your goals while staying grounded in what you already have. It's about finding peace in the present without losing your drive to grow. It's living with purpose, without losing sight of what's important.

How's your work/life balance? The pursuit to provide vs. the pursuit to be home with your family? Only you can reflect on the truth here.

98

Parenting Is Hard for Good Parents

As parents, we often pour immense effort into nurturing our children. And while on the one hand we feel how worthwhile this effort is, it also can lead to stress, guilt, and the constant balancing act of meeting our children's needs while cultivating independence, setting boundaries, and managing work. It's a heavy load. The exhaustion you feel? It's not a sign of weakness or failure. It's a reflection of your commitment, your love, and your unwavering desire to do right by your children.

I remind myself: As parents, we can't perform at our best when we have an empty cup, even if sometimes we have no choice. Self-care is not selfish; it's an essential part of being a good parent. If you are feeling stressed, worn down, burned out, or overwhelmed, you don't have to sacrifice getting to a better place just because your kids have needs as well.

In the movie *Inside Out,* the main character is Riley, a young girl whose emotions are personified as Joy, Sadness, Anger, Fear, and Disgust. She struggles to adjust when her family moves to a new city. Her parents, overwhelmed by their own stress, try their best to support her while maintaining an optimistic front.

One key moment comes when Riley's parents finally acknowledge the weight of the changes they've all been facing. This honest moment of vulnerability allows them to connect as a family. The movie shows that when Riley's parents take care of their own emotional needs and validate their own struggles, they are better equipped to support Riley's journey through hers.

You are not failing your children by admitting you're tired, stressed, or even unsure. You are showing them how to navigate life's challenges with resilience and self-compassion. In fact, modeling self-care is one of the greatest lessons you can teach them.

The next time you feel overwhelmed, remember that it's okay to take a step back. Let your kids see you rest, reflect, and recharge. Show them that being a good parent doesn't mean being perfect—it means being present, patient, and kind, not just to them but to yourself. Be kind to your mind, good parent. You deserve it, and so do they.

***Do you feel like a good parent today?
Reflect on your answer, and, either way,
find a few minutes for yourself today.***

99

Redefining Masculinity

In today's world, fathers are redefining masculinity—both in how they portray it and in how they are raising their sons.

I grew up, like many men today, in a household where my father didn't show much affection. A big hug was rare and reserved for significant goodbyes. Kisses on the cheek were nearly nonexistent, and an occasional "Love you, son," was delivered quickly.

Masculinity is a buzzword in today's society—a term that holds many definitions depending on whom you ask. By definition, *masculinity* refers to the qualities or attributes regarded as characteristic of men or boys. Naturally, opinions on what those characteristics should include vary. Can a man be strong yet gentle? Can a man be assertive yet admit when he's wrong? Can a man excel in leadership but also acknowledge his weaknesses? Regardless of the definition we hold, one truth should unite us: We all want our boys to feel loved by their fathers.

I am raising a son. Maybe you are too, or you have a nephew or godson or boy you are mentoring. With this comes the responsibility of how to raise these boys to be men in the world. So now the million-dollar question: How?

I love showering my son with hugs, telling him all the time how much I love him and am proud of him, and making space for the variety of emotions he expresses. He's young now but I plan to continue this throughout his life.

Let's teach the next generation of boys to embrace their emotions and discover the gentle art of emotional regulation. We can recognize a boy's natural resilience but also understand that it's not his defining characteristic. Let's guide our sons—teaching them to stand up for what's right, treat women with respect, and prioritize a healthy mind.

In a world that often demands increased toughness in men, let's take a different path. There is space for both strength and compassion, like a flickering candle flame as well as a blazing fire. As we nurture the flame of strength and compassion in our sons, we kindle hope for a future where love and understanding light the path forward—together.

If you parent a son, how can you help him nurture compassion? If you parent a daughter, how can you remind her of her strength, worth, and what respect she demands?

100

Take the Adventure

Adventure is worthwhile in itself.
—Amelia Earhart

Most children have an adventurous spirit. I once made a video where my daughter asked if we were going on an adventure (a vacation), and I responded, "Yes, we are!" She jumped up and down frantically and ran out of the room. I showed various slow-motion shots of my kids exploring, and then it cut to black. The text overlay read: "Take the adventure . . ." The video then cut to a shot of me asking my (fictional) now grown-up daughter if she's ready, mentioning that the car was all packed up, as we get ready to leave for college. It cut to black again, reading: "Before the adventure takes them." These adventures do end. Not indefinitely—I know plenty of grown-ups who still adventure with their families. However, there's something magical about that adventurous spirit when our kids are young, the excitement and the sheer simplicity of it.

Adventure is a necessity for living and it's worth instilling in our kids from the start. It doesn't have to mean conquering the tallest mountain in the world, nor does it mean learning how to BASE jump. Adventure looks different for everyone. You don't need to *be* adventurous to *adventure*.

We are all on a spinning rock traveling through space in a universe we have no idea how large—yet we are obsessed with man-made constructs. We don't even realize we haven't watched a sunset in fifteen days because "I have worries I need to worry about." Guilty as charged, but think about it: We often pay more attention to the talking heads who throw nonsense on our screens than to full moons, stars, or a beautiful hill we could hike up with our families. Ground yourself in this thinking every once in a while, it's necessary for life.

Take the adventure.

When's the last time you went on an adventure with your family?

A Final Word

Create Your Story

These reflections are meant to help you understand more about yourself—as both the father you are and the father you want to become. As you made your way through the book, what stood out to you? Did anything come up that you hadn't even realized you'd been doing, maybe a truth you'd internalized that you're finally taking a good look at? Whatever it may be, this is your opportunity to notice and do something about it.

And now it's time to create your story. What's going to be your legacy?

This book is about living in the present, enjoying the time we have with our families, so I don't want you to dwell too much on the future—we aren't even promised it. But looking ahead can help clarify how we are living now and identify if there are any parts we'd like to change while we still have the chance to do so.

Look at your life so far. If you were to write it down

as a story, what would be its main themes? Would you be excited to type out the words, the sentences, the paragraphs that make up the details and events of your life? If not, why? What are the highlights? What challenges have you faced? What do you spend the majority of your time doing? What are you like to be around? How would your kids describe you?

In 2007, author Randy Pausch received devastating news that he had terminal cancer, which meant that he'd be leaving behind his wife and three young children. Asked to give a "last lecture" at Carnegie Mellon University, he embraced the opportunity to impart his personal and professional legacy, something he then recorded in a fantastic book called *The Last Lecture.*

Let me ask you: **What's your last lecture?**

Thankfully, most of us won't have to face down death to gain insights that set our life on the right path. But use it to set perspective, to guide you toward living each day purposely, spending time on the things that matter most. If you wish something were different, now is the time to make a change!

I'm not going to end this book on a morbid note. I can't leave you like that. **Life is beautiful, Dads.** We are alive. And we are raising incredible human beings. What an honor that is, to get to play a part in who they will become, to get to teach them, cheer them on, comfort them, and watch them bloom.

We have an incredible opportunity to be the greatest generation of fathers this world has ever seen. Too often, we diminish ourselves—reducing fatherhood to a supporting role. We sit in the corner, believing the stereotypes and archetypes we've been fed our entire lives. But we have the power to rewrite the script. To change the narrative of what it means to be a dad, a "man of the house," a leader.

We can carry forward the best lessons from the past while also forging a new path. We can support one another. We can share our vulnerabilities. We can break down barriers we once feared, free of judgment or criticism. We can burn the outdated literature that has told us who we are and what we're supposed to be. We can kill the buzzwords and trendy labels that box us in.

We are in control of the future, Dads.

We can achieve our visions. We can build careers that keep us close to our families rather than pull us away. We can laugh at the outdated media portrayal of the clueless dad. We can stop the "mom vs. dad" debates that turn parenting into a competition instead of a partnership. We can make healthy choices for our physical and mental health, we can put habits in place that allow us to show up as the best versions of ourselves. We can put away the distractions and focus on what's in front of us.

We can be the change. Not because society tells us to, but because we tell society.

The world moves in the direction of those who demand change. And we have the power to shape our families, and, by doing so, to create a future through this next generation that is good.

We don't have to believe the narratives that don't serve us.

We can use our words, our actions, and our presence

to change the course of history. If you don't believe that yet, start today.

Believe in yourself.

Create a life you are proud of.

Write a story you are proud of.

You didn't think I'd end the book without giving you one last '90s pop culture reference, did you? In 1991, my favorite childhood movie came out: *Hook*. Robin Williams plays Peter Pan—only now, Peter has grown up to become a workaholic who has lost sight of what truly matters. In one of the best scenes, Peter's wife, Moira, throws his cell-phone out the window after he yells at his children when they interrupted a work call because they were trying to play with him. Moira says: "We have a few special years with our children . . . and you are missing it."

At eight years old, I loved *Hook* because it was a fun adventure story. Now, at forty, I watch it with a whole new perspective.

We know the truth.

We are stepping up. We will step up.

We don't want to miss it.

Dads, we know the story we want to create. And I'm here to tell you—it's possible. You deserve it.

What story will your children tell their children? What story will your children tell the world? When I look ahead to the end of my life, I want to hear my children say these words:

"He was the best dad I could've asked for."

You are a good dad. All the time, energy, money, and effort that you are investing in your kids is important. It can be hard in the daily grind to see it, but you are doing a great job. Keep going.

And with that, I'll leave you with one last quote:

> To live would be an awfully big adventure.
>
> —Peter Pan (*Hook*)

Acknowledgments

Jessica, thank you for believing in me when no one else did and for helping to bring out the best version of me. Thank you for supporting me through every up and down, listening to me in my darkest moments, encouraging me to believe in myself, to chase my dreams, to take risks, and to become my most authentic self. Thank you for being the best mom to our children, for breaking generational curses, and for giving them the love, support, and childhood they deserve. I love you—forever and always.

Dakota Lynn, you amaze me every single day. I'm so proud of the person you are, the kindness you show others, your empathy, and the creativity and effort you put into everything you do. Shoot for the stars, baby girl. Don't let anyone tell you what you can't do. I hope to always be everything you need in a dad. *Nirvana smiley.*

Asher Ridge, I can't wait to see the man you become. I will always be here for you, and I hope you know how special you are. Always follow your dreams. You can do anything you set your mind to. I'm so grateful for you, son. Never stop being yourself. *Roots Bloody Roots.*

Dad, I hope I made you proud with this. I will always

carry with me the example you set with your character, integrity, and the way you shine your light in this world. You once told me I'd be a writer one day, and I guess this is the day you were talking about. Thank you for being my dad. I love you.

Without the people mentioned above, this book would not exist.

To all my followers and supporters of The Tired Dad—thank you. For years, you've supported my work and allowed me to support my family by doing what I love. I've never seen you as just a number, and your messages have never gone unnoticed. I'm grateful for each and every one of you.

My love for writing began early. I owe it to the stories, movies, and music that influenced and inspired me to never give up on this dream. Thank you to the writers of Scary Stories to Tell in the Dark, Goosebumps, *One Flew Over the Cuckoo's Nest, The Great Gatsby, Lord of the Flies, To Kill a Mockingbird,* and *The Grapes of Wrath.*

To the people who created the films *Good Will Hunting, The Professional, Pulp Fiction, Heat, Requiem for a Dream, Trainspotting, Blow, The Shawshank Redemption, Dead Poets Society, Hook, Rudy, The Nightmare Before Christmas, Braveheart, My Girl, The Sandlot,* and *Gladiator*—thank you for moving me, shaping me, and staying with me.

To the musical artists Nirvana, Eminem, The Cranberries, Elliott Smith, Tracy Chapman, Ben E. King, Tupac Shakur, Metallica, Elton John, Green Day, and Alice in Chains—you've been the soundtrack to this journey.

Thank you, Charles, my fellow metalhead, for bringing

my book cover to life—and for standing by me since day one, always believing in my vision.

Thank you, Joaquin, my fellow tired dad, for so beautifully capturing the moments that tell the story of my fatherhood journey through the years.

Thank you, Ryan Holiday, for your books *The Daily Dad, Stillness Is the Key, The Obstacle Is the Way,* and *Ego Is the Enemy.* They have inspired, motivated, and helped me through so much.

Thank you to Convergent and Penguin Random House for believing in this message and taking a chance on me. To my editor, Katy Hamilton, thank you for bringing out the best in my writing and embracing all my crazy ideas.

Mental Health Resources

Below are a handful of organizations and resources that I have found valuable in getting help. Remember: We all struggle at times, and if you find yourself there, it's okay. Reaching out to get help is the strongest thing you can do, for yourself and for your family.

Movember: movember.com
BetterHelp: betterhelp.com
Talkspace: talkspace.com
Psychology Today: psychologytoday.com
The Good Men Project: goodmenproject.com
Dads Matter UK: dadsmatter.org.uk
Mental Health America (MHA): mhanational.org

988 Suicide & Crisis Lifeline

Call or text **988**–24/7, free, confidential mental health support. **United States only**

Crisis Text Line

Text **HOME** or **HOLA** to **741741**—Trained crisis counselors available 24/7 via text. **United States only**

Movies That Have Changed My Parenting Perspective

When it comes to examples of what it looks like to be a good dad, movies have played a big role in my life. The next time you've put the kids to bed and are looking for a good movie to put on, try one of these and be inspired!

Good Will Hunting

The Pursuit of Happyness

Hook

Dead Poets Society

Arrival

Kramer vs. Kramer

Life Is Beautiful

Father of the Bride and *Father of the Bride Part II*

Minari

Mrs. Doubtfire

Marriage Story

Beautiful Boy

I Am Sam

Interstellar

Boyhood

Tully

Gifted

PHOTOGRAPHY BY JOAQUIN RODRIGUEZ, JOAQUINFILMS.COM

Jon Gustin is the founder and owner of The Tired Dad LLC. As a content creator and influencer who goes by the moniker The Tired Dad online, Jon has amassed over two million followers for his portrayal of life as an ordinary father and the lessons he's learned. His videos and writing showcase both the heartwarming and heartbreaking aspects of being a dad. Jon is also the co-host (along with his wife, Jessica) of *The Tired Dad & Tired Mom Podcast*. He and his wife live in Tennessee with their son and daughter.

tireddad.com
Substack: thetireddad.substack.com
Instagram: @TheTiredDad
YouTube: @TheTiredDad
TikTok: @the.tired.dad
facebook.com/thetireddadlife